"What a great team! A master craft designer join forces to help with the . project ever — our own hearts. This wonderful lab manual includes devotion-sized quotes and daily experiments that will help you be with God through daily interactions with his power and presence."

—GARY W. MOON, MDiv, PhD, professor of psychology
and spirituality at the Psychological Studies Institute
and author of *Falling for God*

"Beware! If you are content with a superficial walk with God, this book will be a nagging irritant. But if you long to go deeper with him—not to memorize Scripture out of duty or to practice your faith out of routine or obligation—read this book! Dallas Willard's theological expertise, combined with Jan Johnson's daily experiments and the Holy Spirit's renewal of your heart, will result in the Christian life you've always wanted."

—CAROL KENT, speaker and author

"No one on the contemporary scene articulates the concepts of spiritual formation and discipleship to Jesus more accurately or more biblically than does Dallas Willard, and no one translates these concepts into everyday experience and practices more helpfully than Jan Johnson. Dare to combine these two, and you have an explosive transforming power—nitroglycerin for the spirit. I see no way to work through these experiments without being radically changed from the inside out."

—HOWARD BAKER, instructor of Christian formation and
chaplain, Denver Seminary; author of *Soul Keeping*

248.4
W692rh

RENOVATION
OF THE HEART
IN DAILY PRACTICE

EXPERIMENTS IN SPIRITUAL
TRANSFORMATION

DALLAS WILLARD AND JAN JOHNSON

NAVPRESS®

BRINGING TRUTH TO LIFE

San Diego Christian College
Library
Santee, CA

OUR GUARANTEE TO YOU

We believe so strongly in the message of our books that we are making this quality guarantee to you. If for any reason you are disappointed with the content of this book, return the title page to us with your name and address and we will refund to you the list price of the book. To help us serve you better, please briefly describe why you were disappointed. Mail your refund request to: NavPress, P.O. Box 35002, Colorado Springs, CO 80935.

The Navigators is an international Christian organization. Our mission is to advance the gospel of Jesus and His kingdom into the nations through spiritual generations of laborers living and discipling among the lost. We see a vital movement of the gospel, fueled by prevailing prayer, flowing freely through relational networks and out into the nations where workers for the kingdom are next door to everywhere.

NavPress is the publishing ministry of The Navigators. The mission of NavPress is to reach, disciple, and equip people to know Christ and make Him known by publishing life-related materials that are biblically rooted and culturally relevant. Our vision is to stimulate spiritual transformation through every product we publish.

Devotions © 2006 by Jan Johnson
Original material from *Renovation of the Heart* © 2002 by Dallas Willard

All rights reserved. No part of this publication may be reproduced in any form without written permission from NavPress, P.O. Box 35001, Colorado Springs, CO 80935.
www.navpress.com

NAVPRESS, BRINGING TRUTH TO LIFE, and the NAVPRESS logo are registered trademarks of NavPress. Absence of ® in connection with marks of NavPress or other parties does not indicate an absence of registration of those marks.

ISBN 1-57683-809-9

Cover design by Disciple Design
Cover illustration by Disciple Design
Creative Team: Don Simpson, Kathy Mosier, Arvid Wallen, Laura Spray

Some of the anecdotal illustrations in this book are true to life and are included with the permission of the persons involved. All other illustrations are composites of real situations, and any resemblance to people living or dead is coincidental.

Unless otherwise identified, all Scripture quotations in this publication are taken from the *New American Standard Bible* (NASB), © The Lockman Foundation 1960, 1962, 1963, 1968, 1971, 1972, 1973, 1975, 1977, 1995. The author's paraphrases and translations are marked as PAR. Other versions used include: the HOLY BIBLE: NEW INTERNATIONAL VERSION® (NIV®), Copyright © 1973, 1978, 1984 by International Bible Society, used by permission of Zondervan Publishing House, all rights reserved; *THE MESSAGE* (MSG). Copyright © 1993, 1994, 1995, 1996, 2000, 2001, 2002. Used by permission of NavPress Publishing Group; the *New Revised Standard Version* (NRSV), copyright © 1989, by the Division of Christian Education of the National Council of the Churches of Christ in the USA, used by permission, all rights reserved; and the *King James Version* (KJV).

Willard, Dallas, 1935-
    Renovation of the heart in daily practice : experiments in spiritual
transformation / Dallas Willard and Jan Johnson.
        p. cm.
    Includes bibliographical references.
    ISBN 1-57683-809-9
    1. Spiritual life--Christianity. 2. Spiritual exercises. 3.
Spiritual
    transformation.   I. Johnson, Jan, 1947-   . II. Title.
    BV4501.3.W5533 2006
    248.4--dc22
    2006019085

Printed in the United States of America

1 2 3 4 5 6 / 10 09 08 07 06

FOR A FREE CATALOG OF NAVPRESS BOOKS & BIBLE STUDIES,
CALL 1-800-366-7788 (USA) OR 1-800-839-4769 (CANADA).

CONTENTS

INTRODUCTION

Sometimes it's not enough just to *read* a book. There are books whose ideas demand we interact with them and soak our souls in them. Such a book is Dallas Willard's *Renovation of the Heart*. It can't be quickly devoured, as we say. It calls for our interaction.

C. S. Lewis talks about "receiving" a book instead of "using" it. A "user" sees reading as a pastime, but a "recipient" rests in the ideas. To receive a book is to explore what is being said and to let the author take you on the bicycle ride of your life.[1] You take in all the scenery and let yourself be challenged. You respond to God about what you've read. When you receive a book in this way instead of just using it, it adds to your life.

This book you hold is designed to help you interact with the rich material in *Renovation of the Heart* in a few specific ways. First, you get to see how someone else has interacted with it. Each selection from *Renovation of the Heart* is followed by my description of how one might process the content and what it might look like to walk it out.

Each of my entries also includes "Today's Experiment," which varies from engaging in simple activities you might use to explore the ideas (often interpersonal or physical activities) to interacting with God's written Word in a right-brain imaginative way (to help you hear God) to pondering a few reflective questions. These "experiments" are not hard work; in fact, many are fun. If you don't resonate with a particular exercise, you can tweak it to fit who you are.

You may want to get a spiral notebook for the purpose of doing the exercises and responding to God. Don't be intimidated by the idea of journaling. Call it "scribbling" if you like. If possible, begin by addressing God, but don't be afraid to be exactly who you are in your scribbling. Engagement in open, honest, back-and-forth conversation with God is what I hope this book will inspire.

This book also invites you to interact with *Renovation's* ideas by jotting down notes as you go along. These aren't notes like the ones you took in school, but "notes to yourself"—deep yet practical things you don't want to forget. These notes may actually become part of your interaction with God. So I invite you to underline phrases in this book that speak to you. You may want to consider marking the text in this way:

star = *key ideas* to remember

your initials = *next steps* for you

Be open to God speaking to you, even in the smallest phrases. An idea may be a key one for you because you've been hearing it from God in several ways during the last year. And if you reread the book two or three years from now, you may mark different things.

You may even want to keep a "favorite phrase" list of the ideas that spoke most deeply to you. If so, go back to this list often. Pray about those ideas and discuss them with friends.

My goal is that you will truly interact with God—not just read a book.

KINGDOM POSSIBILITIES

When we open ourselves to New Testament writings and absorb our minds and hearts in one of the Gospels or in letters such as Ephesians or 1 Peter, we get the impression we are looking into another world and another life. It is a divine world and a divine life. Leaping out from the pages are amazing promises to those who give their life to this new world through their confidence in Jesus. For example, Jesus said that those who give themselves to him will receive "living water," the Spirit of God himself. He will keep them from ever again being thirsty—being driven and ruled by unsatisfied desires (see John 4:14). Indeed, they will receive "rivers of living water" flowing from the center of their life to a thirsty world (John 7:38, NRSV).

Paul prayed that believers will "know the love of Christ that surpasses knowledge, so that they may be filled with all the fullness of God . . . by the power at work within us, that is able to accomplish abundantly far more than all we can ask or imagine" (Ephesians 3:19-20, PAR). Peter said that those who love and trust Jesus will "rejoice with an indescribable and glorious joy" (1 Peter 1:8, NRSV), with "genuine mutual love" pouring from their hearts (1:22, NRSV), ridding themselves of "all malice, and all guile, insincerity, envy, and all slander" (2:1, NRSV). As if that weren't enough, these believers would silence scoffers of the Way of Christ by simply doing what is right (see 2:15) and casting all their anxieties upon God because he cares for us (see 5:7).

Ordinary people have entered this kingdom of God and are entering this divine world and divine life even now. It is a world that seems open to us and beckons us to enter. We feel its call.

We often say, "Nobody's perfect." We don't say this just when someone fails but also when we run up against the Bible's description of the kingdom personality of "genuine mutual love" that is free of "all malice, and all guile, insincerity, envy, and all slander." Perhaps we rush to say it because we feel inadequate compared to such love. But what if we don't make that description about us—focusing on our shortcomings—but instead linger on the beauty of God and God's kingdom?

Is it possible we rush to say, "Nobody's perfect" because we've met so few people who show genuine love and move through life without superiority, insensitivity, or gossip? Maybe we have met a few but didn't notice the beauty of their Christlikeness. Instead, we were impressed by other things—their ability to quote Bible verses or answer questions about world religions. Those who speak articulately about the Bible may draw our attention more than those who live a transformed life.

Try picturing this hypothetical moment of dwelling on the beauty of God and the kingdom life: Let's say I confessed to you my disgust with someone who annoyed me and how hopeless I felt about ever loving this person. What if instead of trying to make me feel better by saying, "Nobody's perfect," you said you believed in God's power to transform me into a radical person who pays loving attention to those who annoy me? What if you prayed for me about this? What if later that day you encountered an annoying person and, without thinking, treated that person with kindness and attentiveness—partly because of the transforming effect of our conversation about the kingdom personality?

⟶ TODAY'S EXPERIMENT ⟵

Read slowly these phrases describing the kingdom life and personality:

- to know the love of Christ that surpasses knowledge
- to be filled with all the fullness of God

- power at work within us
- able to accomplish abundantly far more than all we can ask or imagine
- rejoice with an indescribable and glorious joy
- genuine mutual love pouring from their hearts
- without malice, guile, insincerity, envy, and slander

Thank God for the beauty of the kingdom life and for the possibility of the transformation of your soul. Spend a minute or two longing for the kingdom of God in your life: "Thy kingdom come! Thy will be done!"

2

NO UNSOLVABLE PUZZLE

In many historical periods, as well as today, Christians have generally found their way into the divine life slowly and with great difficulty, if at all. Yet formation in Christ is not a mysterious, irrational process, something that strikes like lightning whenever and wherever it will, if at all. It is not something that is magically conferred upon us in the midst of curious rituals and antique practices. Spiritual experiences (such as Paul's on the Damascus road) do not constitute spiritual formation, though sometimes they can be a meaningful part of it.

One reason so many people *fail to immerse themselves in the words of the New Testament* (see quotations in previous devotion) is that the life they see there is so unlike what they know from their experience. This is true even though they may be quite faithful to their church and really do have Jesus Christ as their hope. The New Testament presentation of the life in Christ only discourages them or makes them feel hopeless.

Why should this be so? Surely the life God holds out to us in Jesus was not meant to be an unsolvable puzzle! But this is my observation: For all our good intentions and strenuous methods, we do not *approach and receive that divine life in the right way.* We do not comprehend and convey the wisdom that Jesus and the Bible give us about the nature of human beings and our redemption from the destructive powers that occupy us. Consider these other ideas:

- *It isn't true that where there is a will there is automatically a way* (though, of course, will is crucial). We also need an understanding of exactly what needs to be done and how it can be accomplished.

- *Spiritual formation in Christ is an orderly process.* Although God can triumph in disorder, that is not his choice. And instead of focusing on what God can do, we must humble ourselves to accept the ways he has *chosen* to work with us. Those are clearly laid out in the Bible.

As I visited a missionary friend who was working hard to revive dying churches, I asked him about his plans for discipleship. "Just get people in the church door," he told me. "Then they'll catch on." This reminded me of the old saying that going into a church doesn't make you a Christian any more than going into a garage makes you a car. I thought of all the hostile board meetings, church splits, and personal insults I'd witnessed among people who had been "in the church door" a long time. I stood there and prayed, "O God, give us all a vision and a plan for the transformation of souls."

❧ TODAY'S EXPERIMENT ❧

As you venture into a journey of spiritual formation through this book, consider your vision and plan for the formation of your soul. What do you already know about how God is forming your soul? Make some notes about this as you begin the journey through this book.

What do you think of the following ideas about soul transformation?

- *Immerse yourself in the words of the New Testament.* What would it look like to experience Scripture passages and taste and see that God is good? What ways of being in the Word (with certain people, using certain methods) help you hear God speaking to *you*?
- *"Where there's a will, there's a way" is not true.* When have you strained to become a better person, relying on your will alone? What techniques (such as berating yourself) have you used to force yourself to try to act like Jesus?
- *Spiritual formation in Christ is an orderly process.* Confess to

any beliefs you might have that spiritual growth will somehow just happen without your paying any attention to it. Consider what God has done (what has happened) that has facilitated the most growth in you. How did you cooperate in this?

Pray as you are led. Ask God to show you today the small steps in your life that would quietly and certainly lead to inner transformation.

3

CHANGE ME ON THE INSIDE

O ur lives are a result of what we have become in the depths of our being—what we call our spirit, will, or heart. From there we see our world and interpret reality. From there we make choices, break forth into action, and try to change our world. That is why the greatest need of collective humanity is the renovation of our heart.

Accordingly, the revolution of Jesus involves the objective of eventually bringing all of human life under the direction of his wisdom, goodness, and power as part of God's eternal plan for the universe. The revolution of Jesus is one of *character*, which proceeds by *changing people from the inside* through an ongoing personal relationship to God in Christ and to one another. It changes their ideas, beliefs, feelings, habits of choice, bodily tendencies, and social relations. From these persons, social structures will naturally be transformed so that "justice roll[s] down like waters, and righteousness like an ever-flowing stream" (Amos 5:24, NRSV). Such streams *cannot* flow through corrupted souls.

Spiritual formation for the Christian refers to the Spirit-driven *process of forming the inner world of the human self so that it becomes like the inner being of Christ himself.* To the degree in which spiritual formation in Christ is successful, the outer life of the individual becomes a natural outflow of the character and teachings of Jesus. Christian spiritual formation is focused entirely on Jesus. Its goal is conformity to Christ that arises out of an inner transformation accomplished through purposeful interaction with the grace of God in Christ. Obedience is an essential outcome of Christian spiritual formation (see John 13:34-35; 14:21).

If Christ's people genuinely enter Christ's way of the heart, they will find a sure path toward becoming the persons they were meant to be: thoroughly good and godly persons yet purged of arrogance, insensitivity, and self-sufficiency. Christian assemblies will become what they have been in many periods of the past and what the world desperately calls for today: incomparable schools of life—life that is eternal in quality now, as well as unending in quantity.

When we say phrases such as, "He caught me off guard," or, "That bad word just slipped out," we refer to the truth that our outer actions aren't accidental—they mirror our character within. When regrettable words "slip out," we didn't have time to dress up what was in our heart before it came tumbling out of our mouth. Unsavory thoughts leak out in objectionable words and behavior. Such "slips" reveal publicly the private inner workings of our heart. Jesus explained that "out of the overflow of his heart his mouth speaks" (Luke 6:45, NIV).

Our task, then, is to cooperate with God in being changed on the inside so that we take on the personality of Christ. As we let what is stored in our heart be transformed, we behave as Jesus would behave.

If our insides are renovated, what comes out of us will bring about peace and righteousness. We won't have to *try* to love. Unloving thoughts and actions simply won't occur to us, just as loving ones will begin to spring up without our awareness. We'll smile at an enemy automatically. It won't occur to us to argue. Instead, we'll pray inwardly for the disagreeable person in front of us. To cooperate with public greed or dishonesty will offend us to the core, and we'll find ourselves unable to do it.

⤴ TODAY'S EXPERIMENT ⤵

What sort of heart would you like to have? Dream big: patient, kind, not self-seeking, not easily irritated (see 1 Corinthians 13:4-5). What actions would flow from such a large heart? Close your eyes and think about these things.

Form these dreams and desires into a prayer. If such dreams scare you, admit that to God. Will I get my needs met? Will I be walked on? If you have these fears, admit them to God and ask him for courage. Plead with God to change you on the inside. Picture yourself as one through whom "justice [can] roll down like waters, and righteousness like an ever-flowing stream" (Amos 5:24, NRSV).

4

TRYING TO BE GOOD

The *external* manifestation of Christlikeness is not the *focus* of Christian spiritual formation. When outward forms or behaviors are made the main emphasis, the process will be defeated, falling into deadening legalisms. This has happened in the past, and it is a major barrier to wholeheartedly embracing spiritual formation in the present. Peculiar modes of dress, behavior, and organization are just not the point.

Externalism, as we might call it, was a danger in New Testament times. But "that Christ be formed within you" is the eternal watchword of Christian spiritual formation (Galatians 4:19, PAR). This word is fortified by the deep moral and spiritual insight that while "the letter of the law kills, the spirit gives life" (2 Corinthians 3:6, PAR).

To illustrate briefly, Jesus' teachings in the Sermon on the Mount (see Matthew 5–7) refer to various wrong behaviors: acting out anger, looking to lust, heartless divorce, verbal manipulation, returning evil for evil, and so forth. To strive merely to *act* in conformity with Jesus' expressions of what living from the heart in the kingdom of God is like is to attempt the impossible.

The outward interpretation of spiritual formation (emphasizing specific *acts*) aims to increase "the righteousness of the scribe and Pharisee," but this will not "go beyond" (Matthew 5:20, PAR) to achieve genuine transformation of *who I am* through and through—that is, Christ's man or woman, living richly in his kingdom.

But Christlikeness in the inner being is not a human attainment. It is, finally, a gift of grace. Spiritual formation is the way of rest for the weary and overloaded, of the easy yoke and light burden (see Matthew

11:28-30), of cleaning the inside of the cup and dish (see Matthew 23:26), of the good tree that cannot bear bad fruit (see Luke 6:43). And it is the path along which God's commandments are found not to be heavy or burdensome (see 1 John 5:3).

For some people, coming to faith has felt a bit like a bait-and-switch operation. At first, we hear mostly about grace. We hear we are saved by grace and that salvation is a free gift. But after a while, we are encouraged to try to be good. Yet it is exhausting to try to be good. We think, *This so-called free gift costs more than my puny self can buy. I'll never make it.* Consider the disastrous results of trying to be good. When we seem to be successful at growth, our spirituality becomes about us, not about the power of God in our lives. When we try hard and fail, we berate ourselves and spend tremendous energy on guilt and hopelessness instead of letting ourselves be drawn into the divine life by becoming fascinated with the great example of Jesus in the Gospels.

This weight of trying to be good is an unnecessary load because the way to God is the way of all-encompassing inner transformation. God will work in us (see Philippians 1:6). We have a part in cooperating with God, which is what we'll explore in this book. But even then, we must not make it our *project*. We need to ask God to show us what the next small steps are and how to take them.

❧ TODAY'S EXPERIMENT ❧

Confess any attempts to become like Jesus simply by trying hard to do so. Reflect on the results (or lack of, especially sins that never seem to go away). Consider the energy you have used and the results you've experienced.

Then, feast for a moment on this idea: "Christ in you, the hope of glory" (Colossians 1:27, NIV). Dwell on that thought. If you wish, ask God to do this work within you. Then ask him to show you the next small step (or two or three) you need to make to cooperate in bringing this about in your life. If you're not yet convinced he'll show you, ask him for that faith.

Pray also for Christian groups and their leaders to long for this inner transformation so that Christians can become a touchpoint between heaven and earth.

5

WHO WE ARE, NOT HOW WE ACT

The primary learning in spiritual formation is *not* about how to act, just as the primary wrongness or problem in human life is not what we do. Often what human beings do is so horrible that we can be excused for thinking that all that matters is stopping it. But this is an evasion of the real horror: the heart from which the terrible actions come. In both cases, it is *who we are* in our thoughts, feelings, dispositions, and choices—in the inner life—that counts. Profound transformation there is the only thing that can definitively conquer outward evil.

It is very hard to keep this straight. Failure to do so is a primary cause of failure to grow spiritually. Love is patient and kind (see 1 Corinthians 13:4) so we, mistakenly, try to *be* loving by *acting* patiently and kindly—and we quickly fail. We should always do the best we can in action, of course; but little progress is to be made in that arena until we advance in love itself—the genuine inner readiness and longing to secure the good of others. Until we make significant progress there, our patience and kindness will be shallow and short-lived at best.

It is love itself—*not* loving behavior, or even the wish or intent to love—that has the power to "always protect, always trust, always hope, put up with anything, and never quit" (1 Corinthians 13:7-8, PAR). Merely trying to act lovingly will lead to despair and to the defeat of love. It will make us angry and hopeless.

But *taking love itself—God's kind of love—into the depths of our being through the way of spiritual formation* will, by contrast, enable us to act lovingly to an extent that will be surprising even to us at first. And this love will then become a constant source of joy and refreshment to us and others. Indeed it will, according to the promise, be "a spring of water gushing up to eternal life" (John 4:14, PAR), not an additional burden to carry through life, as the attempt to act lovingly surely would be.

Spiritual formation is the way of those learning as disciples or apprentices of Jesus "to do all things that I have commanded you," within the context of "I have been given say over everything in heaven and earth" and "Look, I am with you every minute" (Matthew 28:18,20, PAR).

You've probably heard people say, "I want patience and I want it now." We laugh because we see how little their character reveals an understanding of the goodness of patience.

As we grow in love—the genuine inner readiness and longing to secure the good of others—patience flows more naturally out of us.

✎ TODAY'S EXPERIMENT ✎

What would it look like for you to "take love itself—God's kind of love—into the depths of your being through the way of spiritual formation"? Consider the following next steps:

- Read through a gospel, pausing to reflect on and relish each loving thing Jesus did.
- Focus on just one loving thing Jesus did and picture his face as he did it. Maybe even put yourself in the place of the person Jesus loved for a moment and absorb that love. And then hold on to that loving look on Jesus' face as you go to sleep tonight.
- Spend a few minutes with the most loving person you know, thanking God the entire time for such a window into the heart of God standing right there next to you.
- Do some small act of service for someone you love who is

feeling overwhelmed: Make his bed, clean her toilet, or make that difficult telephone call he has been dreading.

If you choose to do any of these things (which are examples of the spiritual disciplines of study, meditation, community, and service), do them slowly with the intention of exploring the way God loves in the midst of them. Let that vision of God's love be God's gift to you today.

CHAPTER

6

THE HEART OF ME

The human heart is the executive center of a human life. This is where decisions and choices are made. Heart, spirit, and will refer to the same fundamental component of the person, but they do so under different aspects. Will refers to that component's *power to initiate*, to create, to bring about what did not exist before. Spirit refers to its fundamental *nature* as distinct from physical reality. And heart refers to its *position* in the human being, as the center or core to which every other component of the self owes its proper functioning.

This heart or will or spirit interacts with the six basic aspects of individual human beings.

1. Thoughts (images, concepts, judgments, inferences)
2. Feelings (sensations, emotions)
3. Choice (will, decisions, character)
4. Body (actions, interaction with the physical world)
5. Social context (personal and structural relations to others)
6. Soul (the factor that integrates all of the above to form one life)

David the psalmist, speaking of his own experience, said,

I bless the LORD who gives me counsel;
    in the night also my heart instructs me.
I keep the LORD always before me;
    because he is at my right hand, I shall not be moved.
Therefore my heart is glad, and my soul rejoices;
    my body also rests secure. (Psalm 16:7-9, NRSV)

The ideal is for the whole person to do only what the heart directs. Spiritual formation in Christ is the *process* leading to that ideal, and its result is love of God with *all* of the heart, soul, mind, and strength and love of neighbor as oneself. Each aspect or dimension of the person will be a source of weakness or strength to the whole person, depending on the condition it is in. The condition it is in will depend on the heart. A person who is *prepared* and *capable of* responding to the situations of life in ways that are good and right is a person whose soul is in order, under the direction of a well-kept heart, in turn under the direction of God.

Years ago when I began attending twelve-step meetings, I felt great relief at hearing about the twelve-step goal of "becoming the same person all the time." I felt as if I were many persons. I wanted one thing one minute and another thing the next minute. I wanted to do the right thing, but I also wanted to get unmet needs met, and that might take a little exaggerating or manipulation. Many times I said and did things I later regretted.

With this goal in mind, I began working on having an undivided heart:

> Teach me your way, O LORD,
>   and I will walk in your truth;
> give me an undivided heart,
>   that I may fear your name. (Psalm 86:11, NIV)

To do so, I tried to take all my desires and focus them on God. It took a while to understand that the different aspects of myself needed retraining (reformation or, actually, transformation) before I could follow through to be the same person all the time.

❧ TODAY'S EXPERIMENT ☙

This may sound odd, but experiment with the psalmist's method of talking to his soul:

Why are you in despair, O my soul?
And why have you become disturbed within me?
Hope in God, for I shall again praise Him
For the help of His presence. (Psalm 42:5)

You may wish to use Psalm 16:7-9 to give you ideas of what to say to the various parts of yourself. Here are some ideas to get you started in this dialogue:

- Speak to your mind and feelings, urging them to let the Lord bless them with wise counsel.
- Speak to your heart (will or spirit), asking it to speak to you at night to remind you that "the LORD [is] always before me; because he is at my right hand, I shall not be moved."
- Speak again to your heart and urge it to be glad that the Lord is always before you and you shall not be moved.
- Speak to your soul and urge it to rejoice.
- Speak to your body and reassure it that it can rest secure.

INTERPLAY OF WILL, THOUGHTS, AND FEELINGS

If one's life is to be organized at all, it *must* be organized by the will (or heart or spirit). It can be pulled together from the inside only. The function of the will or heart is to organize our lives as a whole and to organize them around God.

Volition, or choice, is the exercise of will, the capacity of the person to *originate* things and events that would not otherwise occur. By originate I mean to include two of the things most prized in human life: *freedom* and *creativity*. These are really two aspects of the same thing when properly understood: the *power to do what is good* (or evil).

The thought of a sin is not sin, and it is not even a temptation. Temptation is the thought plus the inclination to sin, possibly manifested by lingering over the thought or seeking it out. Without the inner yes, there is no sin. But sin itself is when we inwardly say yes to the temptation, when we *would* do the deed, even though we may not actually get to carry it out.

Yet human life as a whole does not run by will alone. Far from it. Volition is closely intertwined in this process. To choose, one must have some object or concept before the mind and some feeling for or against it. Feeling and thought always go together. They are interdependent and are never found apart. There is no feeling without something being before the mind in thought and no thought without some positive or negative feeling toward what is contemplated.

The person with a well-kept heart is a person who is prepared for and capable of responding to the situations of life in ways that are good and right. This person's will functions as it should—to choose what is good and avoid what is evil—and the other components of his nature cooperate to that end. He need not be perfect, but what all people manage in at least a few times and areas of life, he manages in life as a whole.

When I think, *I must do this*, I've moved beyond feeling to choice (*will*). I have *thought* about this for a long time, and I know I will *feel* regret if I don't do this. These three components of will, thought, and feeling are so closely intertwined that we may not be able to differentiate among them.

Many times we get an inclination to do good, but our thoughts or feelings coax us out of it. Other times we have an inclination to give in to a temptation, but wise thinking or dread of consequences (feelings) help us not to give in.

⌘ TODAY'S EXPERIMENT ⌘

Come before God for the purpose of worship and prayer. Respond to God about this divine idea of giving humans choice, or the ability, to exercise their will. What sort of God is so generous as to share with persons the capacity to *originate* things and events, to exercise freedom and creativity? What sort of God allows humans to move outside his influence with *power to do* what is good or evil? Ponder why God chooses to give us humans such freedom.

As you are ready, offer thoughts to God, such as this:

Oh, the depth of the riches of the wisdom and knowledge of God!
    How unsearchable his judgments,
    and his paths beyond tracing out!
Who has known the mind of the Lord?
    Or who has been his counselor?
Who has ever given to God,

that God should repay him?
For from him and through him and to him are all things.
To him be the glory forever! Amen. (Romans 11:33-36)

8

THE LOUDEST VOICE
WITHIN ME

As our choices settle into character traits, they are "farmed out" to our body, where they occur more or less automatically without our having to think about what we are doing. But because we are trained in a world of wrongness and evil, the body comes to act wrongly before we think and has motions of sin in its members, as Paul said (see Romans 7:23), which may thwart the true intent of our spirit or will by leaping ahead of it. Good intentions alone do not ensure proper action. This is marked by Jesus' words: "The spirit is willing, but the flesh is weak" (Matthew 26:41). In this state, the body dictates to our soul (our executive center), which dictates to the mind and feelings, then to our spirit, and back to God. Conversely, the "life from above" flows the opposite way: from God to the spirit, to our mind and feelings, to our soul, and then to our body and its social context.

The former order (in which the body dictates) is characteristic of what Paul described as "the mind set on the flesh," which is "death." The latter expresses "the mind set on the Spirit," which is "life and peace" (Romans 8:6). The "flesh" refers to the *natural human powers or capabilities*. But for the individual away from God, flesh becomes, in practice, simply the body. If we focus on our body as our main concern, we make it impossible to please God, and we ensure the utter futility of our lives.

"For those who are according to the flesh [the *natural human powers only*] set their minds on the things of the flesh, but those who are according to the Spirit, the things of the Spirit. For the mind set on the flesh is death, but the mind set on the Spirit is life and peace, because the mind set on the flesh is hostile toward God; for it does not subject itself to the law of God, for it is not even able to do so" (Romans 8:5-7). The will or spirit, tiny power that it is, is very largely at the mercy of the forces playing upon it from the larger self and beyond.

Do you ever leave a situation and wonder why you said the things you said? Somehow you got "carried away." It's as if the body has a life of its own, and it does. Sin dwells in our members—our tongue, even our hands. Our automatic words and gestures can be death dealing or life giving.

This becomes real to us when we try to stop doing certain things. For example, those who interrupt others as they speak struggle to stop doing this. Without realizing it, they have trained their body—specifically their mouth—to speak forth what the mind is thinking with little regard for the person they're talking to. They routinely and with a clear conscience silence the other person's voice.

That's where spiritual disciplines help. For example, the discipline of silence—especially the mini-discipline of letting others have the last word (not one-upping them or defending ourselves)—teaches our body to be at rest, to hear people and appreciate them as they speak. We may also need to add the discipline of prayer, to pray for the person as he or she speaks.

↢ TODAY'S EXPERIMENT ↣

Observe the habits that dwell in your body: not looking at people when they speak to you, interrupting them (if not aloud, then in your head), looking around at other people when someone speaks to you, shutting down when certain people speak to you, pacing or wagging your finger at people when you get wound up about a topic. Reflect on the inner qualities that must exist in the various aspects of you and how they do or don't dictate to your body. If you were to use your body to love God and others as yourself, what sort of retraining would the different parts of you need?

POSSESSING THE LAND

The body, as well as the other aspects of the individual, can be re-formed to become our ally in Christlikeness. How?

The land promised to the Israelites was one of incredible goodness—"flowing with milk and honey," as it is repeatedly described. But it *still had to be conquered by careful, persistent, and intelligent human action* over a long period of time.

In the beginning of the conquest of the Promised Land, the walls of Jericho fell down to make clear God's presence and power. But that never happened again. The Israelites had to take the remaining cities through hand-to-hand warfare, though always with divine assistance.

What was then true of the Promised Land of the Israelites is true of individual human beings who come to God. The Israelites were saved or delivered by grace just as surely as we are. But in both cases, grace means we are to be—and God enables us to be—active to a degree we have never been before. Paul's picture of grace is this: "And God is able to make all grace abound to you, so that always having all sufficiency in everything, you may have an abundance for every good deed" (2 Corinthians 9:8).

We therefore live in "hot pursuit" of Jesus Christ. "My soul followeth hard after thee," the psalmist called out (63:8, KJV). And Paul's panting cry was, "That I may know him, and the power of his resurrection, and the fellowship of his sufferings, being conformed to his death in order to participate in the life of his resurrection" (Philippians 3:10-11, PAR). What are we to say of those who think they have something more important to do than that? The work of spiritual formation in

Christlikeness is the work of claiming the land of milk and honey in which we are, individually and collectively, to dwell with God.

It's quite startling to begin to believe that transformation into Christlikeness is really possible. You and I really could become persons who are kind to our enemies, who listen attentively to the people who annoy us, who work tirelessly to help others without hoping to get any credit.

To possess this promised land of transformation, we will have to arrange our lives differently. As we become more interested in this, we may find ourselves inadvertently giving up the hours we used to spend shopping. We will look forward to reading the Gospels and picturing the selfless, luminous person of Jesus whom even government embezzlers loved to have dinner with. We will be transfixed by seeing Jesus in the midst of his world loving his enemies—exuding love even as he washed the feet of his betrayer, Judas.

Such transformation is possible. God will do this—make all grace abound to us, that always having all sufficiency in everything, we may have an abundance for every good deed. God will direct us in our cooperative efforts to possess this land. For now, the question is this: Do I believe transformation can happen? Am I conscious during the moments of my day that everything I do can contribute to this if I have an understanding and willingness of how spiritual formation works?

ᴄ᙭ TODAY'S EXPERIMENT ᙭ᴐ

Speak to God about this possibility. If you need to express honest doubts that you could ever be formed into Christlikeness, do so. Tell God what you admire most about Jesus and what you would most like to be able to do in cooperation with the power of the Spirit. Thank God for the opportunity to explore this transformation process.

RUINED SOULS

One of the greatest obstacles to effective spiritual formation in Christ today is our failure to understand and acknowledge the reality of the human situation. We must start from where we really are.

Some years back, within a period of a few weeks, three nationally known pastors in Southern California were publicly exposed for sexual sins. But sex is far from being the only problem inside and outside the church. The presence of vanity, egotism, hostility, fear, indifference, and downright meanness can be counted on among professing Christians. Their opposites cannot be counted on or simply assumed in the standard Christian group, and the rare individual who exemplifies these opposites—genuine purity and humility, death to selfishness, freedom from rage and depression, and so on—will stand out in the group with all the obtrusiveness of a sore thumb. This person will be a constant hindrance in group processes and will be personally conflicted by them, for he or she will not be living on the same terms as the others.

Paul described the human self:

"There is none righteous, not even one;
There is none who understands,
There is none who seeks for God;
All have turned aside, together they have become useless;
There is none who does good,
There is not even one."
"Their throat is an open grave,
With their tongues they keep deceiving,"

"The poison of asps is under their lips";
"Whose mouth is full of cursing and bitterness";
"Their feet are swift to shed blood,
Destruction and misery are in their paths,
And the path of peace they have not known."
"There is no fear of God before their eyes." (Romans 3:10-18)

Paul summed up the root of human evil by saying, "There is no fear of God before their eyes." When God is put out of the heart and the soul, the intellect becomes dysfunctional, trying to devise a "truth" that will be compatible with the basic falsehood that not God, but rather man, is god; and the affections (feelings, emotions, even sensations) soon follow along on the path to chaos.

The path of spiritual transformation today lies *through* the illumination that we have ruined souls. This must be gratefully and humbly accepted and applied, to oneself above all. When the prophet Jeremiah, for example, said,

"The heart is more deceitful than all else
And is desperately sick;
Who can understand it?" (17:9),

we have to recognize from our heart that *we* are the ones spoken of, that, indeed, *I* am the one described. Only then is a foundation laid for spiritual formation into Christlikeness.

Think about someone you have known who exemplified genuine purity and humility, selflessness, freedom from rage and depression. Usually such folks have none of the Christian "celebrity" trappings about them. They are often overlooked, even by Christians. They may ask questions no one wants to address, but it's hard to dismiss them because they can ask these questions with gentleness and kindness. They are not living on the same terms as the general culture, and so others might find this confusing.

☙ TODAY'S EXPERIMENT ☙

Contact such a person, if possible. Or contact someone who knew that person well. Ask questions such as, "What is the most important thing to you? Why isn't it important to you to be the center of attention? What advice would you give me?"

If such contact isn't possible, journal for a few moments about one of these things:

- What attracted you to that person? Did you dismiss this person, as others may have?
- Ask God to show you what you need to know about yourself.
- Have you perhaps been this selfless now and then? If so, what precipitated it?

Then speak to God about your ruined soul: the lack of genuine purity, humility, and selflessness, and the existence of rage and depression. Thank God for the picture of Jesus Christ given in the New Testament and for the fact that Jesus makes it possible for us to be transformed.

11

GOD BEING GOD

The fear of God, the proverb tells us, is the beginning of wisdom, and *knowledge of the Holy One* is understanding (see Proverbs 9:10). "Knowledge" in biblical language never refers to head knowledge but always to *experiential involvement*. Thus, when Jesus defined eternal life as "that they might *know* thee the only true God, and Jesus Christ, whom thou hast sent" (John 17:3, KJV), he was speaking of the constant, close interaction with the Trinitarian being of God. Jesus brings this grace into the lives of those who seek and find him.

Progressive departure from God leads to life as we know and see it around us. The first of the Ten Commandments deals with this inclination away from God (see Exodus 20:2-3). God being God offends human pride. If God is running the universe and has first claim on our lives, guess who *isn't* running the universe and does not get to have things as they please?

For the person ho does not live honestly and interactively with God, the body becomes the primary area of pleasure and the primary source of terror, torture, and death. "Free love," as it is euphemistically but falsely called, along with the various forms of perversion, is an extension of body worship (see Romans 1:26-27). But sensuality *cannot* be satisfied. That is partly because the effect of engaging in the practices of sensuality is to deaden feeling, which awakens the desperate need simply *to feel*, to feel *something*. We have to have feeling, and it needs to be deep and sustained. But if we are not living the great drama of goodness in God's kingdom, sensuality through the body is all that is left.

The drive for self-gratification opens up into a life where nothing is forbidden—one can do whatever one can get away with. "Why?"

is replaced with "Why not?" And because this is what these "gods" want—total license—God abandons them to a worthless mind: "As they did not see fit to center their knowledge upon God, God released them into the grip of a nonfunctional mind, to do what is indecent" (Romans 1:28, PAR).

Such behavior, if not approved outright, is excused or even justified by clever psychological, legal, and moral maneuvers. This has been the end stage of every successful human society. Invariably, such a society begins to believe *it* is responsible for its success and prosperity and begins to worship itself and rebel against the understandings and practices that allowed it to be successful under God in the first place. But underneath it all is the radical evil of the human heart—a heart that would make *me* God in place of God.

Like many folks, I would not choose the Ten Commandments as my favorite Scripture to cozy up with. But I experienced them differently when I experimented with Martin Luther's way of praying called the Four Golden Strands. He prayed a verse of Scripture in four ways. First, he asked God to help him *apply* the verse to himself in as many ways as possible (strand 1—but note that this is a prayer, not a beating-self-up session). Then he made appropriate *confessions* to God based on those applications (strand 2). He then *thanked* God for anything related to the verse's truth (strand 3). Finally, he offered *requests* of God regarding the truth of that verse.[2]

Since Luther often did this with the Ten Commandments, I decided to give it a try as I was hiking one day. Certainly the first two commandments did not apply to me because I wasn't an idol worshipper, but I started with the first one anyway: "Thou shalt have no other gods before me" (Exodus 20:3, KJV). In the heat and tedium of the steep switchbacks of the trail, I saw that I had an enormous god before God. It was my comfort. Sure, I served, but I arranged service around getting or doing whatever made me comfortable. If circumstances became uncomfortable, I whined to God nonstop. So I confessed this to God and then thanked him for being One who brings us peace and security in what appears to be uncomfortable circumstances (thereby using us in such powerful ways). I asked God to help me trust him for my comfort.

☙ TODAY'S EXPERIMENT ☙

Try praying a verse of Scripture using Luther's Four Golden Strands. If possible, start with the Ten Commandments and see how long you can stay off your knees.

12

THE SOUL'S LOSTNESS

A ruined soul is a *lost* soul. What is a lost soul? Someone God is mad at? Theologically, the *outcome* of lostness is hell—a most uncomfortable notion. Certainly, if you are lost you are not likely to arrive where you want to be. But the *condition* of lostness is not the same as the *outcome* to which it leads. We're not lost because we are going to wind up in the wrong place. We are going to wind up in the wrong place because we are lost.

To be lost means to be *out of place*, to be omitted. *Gehenna*, the term often used in the New Testament for the place of the lost, may be thought of as the cosmic dump for the irretrievably useless. Think of what it would mean to find you have become irretrievably useless. When your car keys are lost, they are useless to you. When we are lost to God, we are not where we are supposed to be in his world and hence are not caught up into his life. We are our own god, and our god doesn't amount to much. To be lost means to be self-obsessed, to mistake one's own person for God. Such a person really does think he is in charge of his life—though to manage it, he may have to bow outwardly to this or that person or power. But *he* is in charge (he believes), and he has no confidence in the one who really is God.

This self-idolatry sees the universe with different eyes. Each is a god unto himself. Thus no one chooses to go to hell or to be the kind of person who belongs there, but his orientation toward himself leads him to become the kind of person for whom away-from-God is the only place for which he is suited. He would choose that place for himself rather than humble himself before God and accept who God is.

We should seriously inquire if to live in a world permeated with God and the knowledge of God is something we truly desire. If not, we can be assured that God will excuse us from his presence. In this case, we have become people so locked into our own self-worship and denial of God that we *cannot want God*. We cannot want God to be God. *Wanting God to be God is very different from wanting God to help us.*

The ruined soul is not one who is mistaken about theological points and flunks a theological examination at the end of life. One does not miss heaven by a hair but *by constant effort to avoid and escape God.*

Someone who had reason to put confidence in himself—and thereby be a lost soul—was the centurion in Capernaum. He came to Jesus asking him to heal his servant who was suffering terribly. Jesus agreed, but the centurion was so *confident in Jesus* that he said, "Lord, I do not deserve to have you come under my roof. But just say the word, and my servant will be healed" (Matthew 8:8, NIV).

Stunning his Jewish listeners, Jesus complimented this Gentile by saying his faith was greater than that of anyone he'd met in Israel. Jesus then launched into a short description of heaven and hell, inverting all their cherished beliefs by saying that many would come from east and west (Gentiles!) for the feast in the kingdom of heaven, but subjects of the kingdom (Jews who relied on their Jewish identity to enter the kingdom) would "be thrown outside, into the darkness, where there will be weeping and gnashing of teeth" (verses 11-12). It's as if Jesus said, "Things are not what they seem. I am the key, and *confidence in me* is what you need."

☙ TODAY'S EXPERIMENT ❧

Let's look at how the centurion presented a picture of the ruined soul's way forward by having complete confidence in Jesus. Read Matthew 8:5-13, first putting yourself in the place of an onlooking disciple. Notice how easily Jesus spoke with a (heathen) Roman centurion.

Allow yourself to be appalled by Jesus' compliment of his faith.

Then read the passage again. This time put yourself in the place of the centurion. What is it like to have such confidence in God? Pray about what you would look like if you had this kind of confidence.

CHAPTER

13

WANTING THAT DIFFERENT KIND OF LIFE

The ruined soul must be willing to recognize its own ruin before it can discover how to enter a different path, the path of eternal life that naturally leads to spiritual formation in Christlikeness. This transformation is not something that may or may not be added on as an *option* to the gift of eternal life. It is the path one must be on in order to have an eternal kind of life.

This transformation is not a project of "life enhancement," where the life in question is that of "normal" human beings—a life apart from God. It is, rather, the process of developing a *different kind of life*, the life of God himself, sustained by God as a new reality in those who have confidence that Jesus is the anointed One, the Son of God. Those "in Christ"—that is, caught up in his life, in what he is doing, by the inward gift of birth from above—"are of a new making. The 'old stuff' no longer matters. It is the new that counts" (2 Corinthians 5:17, PAR). Here in this new creation is the radical goodness that alone can thoroughly renovate the heart.

To profess Christ today involves little sorrow over who one is, or even for what one has done. Christians commonly speak of their "brokenness," but they are usually talking about their *wounds*, the things they have suffered, not about the evil that is in them.

Few today have discovered that they have been disastrously wrong and cannot change or escape the consequences of their wrongness on their own. There is little sense of "Woe is me! for I am undone; because I am a man of unclean lips, and I dwell in the midst of a people

43

of unclean lips: for mine eyes have seen the King, the LORD of hosts" (Isaiah 6:5, KJV). Yet *without this realization of our utter ruin*, and without the genuine revising and redirecting of our lives that this bitter realization naturally gives rise to, *no clear path to inner transformation can be found.* We will steadfastly remain on the throne of our universe, perhaps trying to "use a little God" here and there.

Becoming a "better Christian" doesn't mean becoming a nicer version of ourselves or getting involved in the local church. Although those things may happen, focusing on such things misses the point. The life from above is a completely different kind of life that may seem odd to others. Building self-esteem or trying to look good doesn't matter anymore. I'm now aware that I'm *not* okay. We're all in serious trouble.

The ones who are immersed in the life of God have a power and character that are strange to this world. They know they are dust (see Psalm 103:14) and have attached themselves to the life that is the "light of men" (John 1:4, NIV).

⚘ TODAY'S EXPERIMENT ⚘

Ponder Isaiah 6:1-8 using your imagination. King Uzziah has just died, so a prophet is needed more than ever. You—a young person, probably related to royalty—see in a vision the Lord seated on a throne that is so high that the tail of the Lord's coat fills up the temple—as if the temple were filled with fog. Creatures with six wings call out, probably echoing each other, "Holy, holy, holy, is the LORD of hosts: the whole earth is full of his glory" (verse 3, KJV). You feel the ground underneath you shake, and you smell smoke all around you (imagine thick smoke from a barbecue or from the smoke machine at a concert).

In response to all this majesty, you understand that you are a ruined soul and that you have tried to maneuver yourself onto that throne. Throwing yourself down, you shout, "Woe is me! for I am undone; because I am a man of unclean lips, and I dwell in the midst of a people of unclean lips: for mine eyes have seen the King, the Lord of hosts" (verse 5, KJV).

Does it surprise you that Isaiah became caught up in the life of God, in what God was doing, and later said, "Here am I; send me" (verse 8, KJV)? Go over this scene several times, preparing yourself for further study about spiritual formation.

14

FOUNDATION FOR SPIRITUAL FORMATION

A shift toward self-denial is needed to reorder the six dimensions of the human self in subordination to God. Self-denial mustn't be confused with self-*rejection*, nor should it be thought of as a painful, strenuous effort against one's will. Instead, it is a settled condition of life in the kingdom of God, better described as "death to self." *Christian spiritual formation rests on this indispensable foundation of death to self and cannot proceed except insofar as that foundation is being firmly laid and sustained.*

We must simply *lose* our lives—those *ruined* lives about which most people complain so much anyway. "Those who have found their life (soul) shall lose it," Jesus said, "while those who have lost their life (soul) for my sake shall find it" (Matthew 10:39, PAR). Our "survival" cannot be the ultimate point of reference in our world. We must not treat ourselves *as* God. This selfless life enables us to do for the first time what we want to do: be truthful, transparent, helpful, and sacrificially loving, with joy. Our lives are then caught up in God's life, a way of "life and peace" (Romans 8:6) because we live from God.

Yet there must be a realism to it. Otherwise one is in danger of falling into the same kind of cheery falseness that characterizes so much current talk of self-esteem. The necessary support for giving and forgiving is abundantly supplied by Jesus through the reality of the kingdom of God that he brings into our lives. He makes this available to us in response to our confidence in him. It is love of God, admiration and confidence in his greatness and goodness, and the regular experience of his care that free us from the burden of looking out for ourselves.

What remarkable changes this introduces into our day-to-day life. At the beginning of my day, I commit my day to the Lord's care while meditatively praying through the Lord's Prayer and possibly the Twenty-Third Psalm. Then I meet everything that happens as sent, or at least permitted, by God. I meet it resting in the hand of his care. I no longer have to manage the weather, airplanes, and people.

The idea of "death to self" is radical in a culture that tells us it's normal to beef up our résumé, exaggerate our successes, and put forward the foot that impresses others most. After we recover from the shock that growing disciples of Jesus are to die to self-promotion, we find it difficult to believe it's possible to live a rich life in God in which we *lack nothing*! We won't have to fake this (having to pretend we don't want to be rich, thin, or own a fancy car). It will be normal because we are caught up in God's life. We really will be okay; in fact, we'll be so much better than we've ever been before.

⨳ TODAY'S EXPERIMENT ⨳

Quiet yourself and try to truly believe the ideas in Psalm 23:1-3. Picture this sheep who is surrounded by green pastures yet isn't on his feet munching away. This sheep is so full and satisfied that he contentedly lies down without needing even a bite. Move through the verses in a way such as this (fill in the blanks with details from your life):

Maybe the Lord really is my shepherd today. Perhaps I really do have everything I need, even when it comes to_____. The Lord will provide me green pastures, even though I may not recognize them at first. I may think that what I need is missing, but it will be there. I'll figure that out faster if I rest (lie down) in God. The still waters are there for me to drink from any minute I need them. In certain events today, such as_____, I may need them frequently.

God is restoring my broken soul today. It is healthier than ever.

When I become confused today, God will guide me in the right path. Again, I may not recognize it until later, but I can trust God's name, God's presence, and God's power in my life today.

What "Death to Self" Looks Like

As our personality becomes reorganized around God and his eternal life, self-denial becomes our settled disposition. At first we self-consciously deny ourselves—reject the preeminence of what *we* want when *we* want it—and look to specific motions of God's grace to guide and strengthen us in this. We will need a wise and constant use of disciplines for the spiritual life. This is because the substance of our selves, formed in a world against God, is *ready* to act otherwise.

When we are dead to self we will not be surprised or offended at not getting what we want. We will not even notice some things that others would react to, such as social slights, verbal put-downs, or physical discomforts. Other rebuffs *will* be noticed, but if we are dead to self to any significant degree, these rebuffs *will not take control* of us or disturb our feelings or peace of mind. As Saint Francis of Assisi said, we will "wear the world like a loose garment, which touches us in a few places and there lightly."

Apprentices of Jesus know that "God causes all things to work together for good to those who love God, to those who are called according to His purpose" (Romans 8:28). They do not have to look out for themselves because they are not in charge of their lives; rather, God is. They appropriately look after things that concern them, but they do not worry about outcomes that merely affect adversely their own desires and feelings. They are free to focus their efforts on the service of God and others and the furthering of good.

Some sensitivity to self will remain, but it will not take over our actions and lives. In my late teens and early twenties, I became quite vain and dependent upon what others thought and said about me. I wanted praise. In time and by God's grace I became *substantially* — not totally — delivered through meditation on Scripture, general studies, solitude, prayer, service to others, and just life experience, along with the movements of grace in my heart and soul. Perhaps I am rarely governed by vanity now — others must be the judge of that — but it is still something I frequently *feel*. And I know that it *could* be something that controls my feelings and behavior were I to let it.

As you ask God to enable you to learn "death to self," you might consider how using disciplines of service, silence, prayer, and meditation may help. *Serving* those who never thank us and doing it for the love of Jesus can retrain us against our desire to be noticed or appreciated. Mini-disciplines of *silence* retrain us, especially ones such as not giving advice unless asked. This thwarts my idea that as a support group leader and platform speaker I know important insights that must be shared! When I don't speak up, however, I end up *praying* for people instead. And finally, *meditating* on passages such as Psalm 23 prepares us to be almost at peace as we practice these other disciplines.

✎ TODAY'S EXPERIMENT ✎

Quiet yourself and then ponder your way through Psalm 23:4-6, perhaps in a way similar to this:

Because I'm beginning to believe the Lord is my Shepherd, I'm not quite as uneasy facing shadowy places in life. At times, I actually have no fear of anything. I see God's hand guiding and comforting me through each detail (see verse 4). In those dramatic moments when I face those who oppose me, dislike me, or just plain annoy me, I find God behind me, pouring love into me, giving me just what I need. Actually, what I need overflows! Now and then I even offer some of that overflow to my enemy (see verse 5). Each day I find goodness and love occurring in the oddest places. Could that be because I no longer demand and expect it from others? I'm content to hang out with Jesus all day long. Whatever he's up to, I want to tag along.

16

STANDING FOR THE RIGHT WITHOUT EGOTISM

One source of difficulty in dying to self is that we may confuse our desire for what is good and right with our desire to *have our own way*. In many controversies, important values are at stake and people are passionately committed to each side. That is as it should be. But more often than not, the contempt and anger that emerges in the conflict manifests the will to have *our* way. Families, churches, communities, and sovereign nations become embroiled in deadly conflicts that would disappear or be resolved but for the relentless will to have our way. "Unless a grain of wheat falls into the earth and dies," Jesus said, "it remains alone; but if it dies, it bears much fruit. He who loves his life [soul] loses it, and he who hates his life in this world will keep it to life eternal" (John 12:24-25).

Does dying to self mean we will be without feeling? Far from it. Apprentices of Jesus become disturbed about many things and passionately desire many things, but not getting their way does not disturb them.

To accept with confidence in God that we do not have to get our own way releases us from the great pressure that anger, unforgiveness, and the "need" to retaliate impose upon our lives. This by itself is a huge transformation of the landscape of our lives. It removes the root and source of the greater part of human evil in our world.

Jesus commanded "not to resist him who is evil; but whoever slaps you on your right cheek, turn to him the other also" (Matthew

5:39, PAR). Such remarkable teaching presupposes that we have laid down the burden of having our own way. We can't begin to even understand it, except from a posture of self-denial based on the confidence and experience of God's all-sufficient presence in our lives. But to step with Jesus into the path of self-denial immediately breaks the ironclad grip of sin over human personality and opens the way to a fuller restoration of radical goodness to the soul. It accesses supernatural strength for life (see Psalm 84:7).

When I first began contemplating "death to self," I nearly became morbid about it. But as I meditated on Scripture passages about this topic, I noticed how each also spoke of being enabled to live a new, eternal kind of life. The grain of wheat dies, but then it *bears much fruit*; disciples of Jesus hate (or prefer God's life over) their life but get to *keep their life for eternal life* (see John 12:24-25). Those who are crucified with Christ and no longer live have Christ *living in them* and *live a life in their body by the faith of the Son of God* (compared to my decrepit faith; see Galatians 2:20). I found that death to self occurs in small steps. Every day I volunteer for small deaths to self, and I experience a little more of that fruit-filled eternal kind of life from above—right here and now on this planet.

After a while, a selfless life begins to make sense. It seems silly to repay evil for evil—what good does that do? Wouldn't it be smarter not to fight fire with fire but with a shocking amount of water? Life becomes more pleasant and interesting. The burdens get lighter and lighter. As I surrender, all is given to me; "a good measure, pressed down, shaken together and running over, will be poured into [my] lap" (Luke 6:38, NIV).

✎ TODAY'S EXPERIMENT ✐

Reflect on situations that bring out the worst sort of self-promotion in you. Do they occur when you're around people who put you down? Who are bossy? Who hold opinions opposite yours? Who look up to you? What could you pray about those situations now, while you're not in the middle of them? What could you pray about the people usually involved, especially to will good in their lives and move toward conformity with Christ?

17

WHAT IS OUR PLAN?

R ecently I learned that one of the most prominent leaders in an important segment of Christian life "blew up," became uncontrollably angry, when someone questioned him about the quality of his work. This was embarrassing, but it is accepted (if not acceptable) behavior; in this case, the one who was questioning him was chastised. That is a familiar pattern in both Christian and non-Christian power structures. What are we to say about the spiritual formation of that leader? The same questions arise with reference to lay figures in areas of life such a politics, business, entertainment, or education who show the same failures of character while openly identifying themselves as Christians. It is unpleasant to dwell on such cases, but they must be squarely faced.

The sad thing when any individual "fails" is not just what he does but also his heart and inner life that are revealed when he does it. We find out who he has been *all along*, what his inner life has been like, and no doubt also how he has suffered during the years before he was found out. What kind of person has he been on the inside, and what has been his relation to God? The effort to change our behavior *without* inner transformation is precisely what we see in the current shallowness of Western Christianity.

If we, through well-directed and unrelenting action, effectually receive the grace of God in salvation and transformation, we certainly will be incrementally changed toward inward Christlikeness. The transformation of the outer life, especially of our behavior, will follow suit. Jesus said that "no good tree produces bad fruit" (Luke 6:43, PAR).

If we are to be spiritually formed in Christ, we must understand

and implement the *general pattern* that all effective efforts toward personal transformation must follow: appropriate *vision, intention,* and *means.* If this VIM pattern is not put in place properly and held there, Christ simply will not be formed in us.

When we do things we later regret—especially when we do them publicly or are found out in some way—we often forge great intentions to change. It's possible the prominent leader mentioned earlier regretted his actions privately but noticed that it was effective when the one who questioned him about it was chastised. He was affirmed in this anger, and the pattern will continue. On the other hand, perhaps he kicked himself for losing his temper and asked God for the umpteenth time to change him. Such regret usually does not change us.

But what if that person met with some folks who loved him, and together they devised some simple disciplines to help him stop managing his world with anger and contempt? Perhaps his vision of life in the kingdom—in which he didn't insist on his own way—would fuel this intention to follow through as he was bolstered by those who loved him. Perhaps he would go on to become someone who invited questioning, and all his endeavors would profit enormously by that.

❧ TODAY'S EXPERIMENT ☙

Reflect for a moment on the things you'd like to see changed about yourself, especially those that would help you reflect the understanding, feelings, decisions, and character of Christ. (You may wish to write these down.) Then ask God for wisdom as you look at your list and ask yourself: What does each item tell me about who I have been *all along*? What has my inner life been like? How have I suffered for this? Tell God what kind of person you would like to be on the inside and what you would like your relationship with him to be like.

18

VIM: VISION OF LIFE IN THE KINGDOM

This vision of the kingdom is where Jesus started and where we must also start. He came announcing, manifesting, and teaching the availability and nature of the kingdom of the heavens. "For I was sent for this purpose," he said (Luke 4:43).

The kingdom of God is the *range of God's effective will, where what God wants done is done.*[3] Earth and its immediate surroundings seem to be the only place in creation where God permits his will to *not* be done. Therefore we pray, "Thy kingdom come, Thy will be done in earth, as it is in heaven" (Matthew 6:10, KJV) and hope for the time when that kingdom will be completely fulfilled even here on earth, where, in fact, it is already present (see Luke 17:21) and available to those who seek it with all their heart (see Matthew 6:33; 11:12; Luke 16:16). For those who seek it, it is true even now that all things work together for their good and that nothing can cut them off from God's inseparable love and effective care (see Romans 8:28,35-39).

The vision that underlies spiritual transformation into Christlikeness is, then, the vision of life now and forever in the range of God's effective will, that is, *partaking* of the divine nature through a birth "from above" and *participating* by our actions in what God is doing now in our lifetime on earth (see 2 Peter 1:4, 1 John 3:1-2). Therefore, we can say, "Whatever we do, speaking or acting, we do all on behalf of the Lord Jesus, giving thanks through him to God the Father" (Colossians 3:17, PAR). In everything we do, we are permitted to do his work. What we are aiming for in this vision is to live fully in the kingdom of God, as fully as possible *now* and *here*, not just hereafter.

One of the benefits of reading the Gospels over and over is how they give us a picture of life in the kingdom of God. Because Jesus operated out of that kingdom, he was so full of compassion and justice that he temporarily suspended his own arrest to lean over and heal the wound of his captor's servant (see Luke 22:51). (Imagine—he could have made his captors disappear.) Out of that kingdom Jesus understood the necessary manipulation of matter, so that walking on water was possible not only for himself but also for a disciple he wished to teach. In many intriguing conversations with him, others saw that he lived out of a place completely different from this planet.

The idea that the kingdom of God is within us, that it is present and available to all who seek it, is one of the most exciting truths of Scripture. Life in this kingdom is possible today as I do mundane things that could bore me, as I work at projects that seem beyond my skills, as I deal with people whose presence reveals my pride or impatience. With this vision of the kingdom, I am released from these earthly shackles and freed to live another kind of life.

Ꮼ Today's Experiment Ꮼ

Read through the first four chapters of a gospel, perhaps John. Look closely at the person of Jesus, especially how he behaved and taught. As you read, think about these questions:

- Where do you spot Jesus living out the kingdom of God—where what God wants done is done—through his teachings, behaviors, and choices of whom to associate with?
- How well did those around him spot the kingdom of God in him?
- What do you learn about the kingdom of God—its nature, powers, and character—from what Jesus did and said?

After you've finished, sit and ponder what fascinates you most about life in the kingdom of God. What touches you? What scandalizes you—makes you gulp hard? What confuses you? Respond to God about these things.

VIM: INTENTION

The problem of spiritual transformation among those who identify themselves as Christians today is not that it is impossible or that means to it are not available. Rather, the problem is that it is not intended. People do not see the value of transformation and decide to carry through with it. They do not decide to do the things Jesus did and said. This is largely due to the fact that they have not been given a vision of life in God's kingdom so that such a decision and intention would make sense. The entire VIM of living the life of Christ is not the intentional framework of their lives. Those who minister to them do not bend every effort to make it so.

The vision of life in the kingdom through reliance upon Jesus makes it possible for us to *intend* to live in the kingdom as he did. We can actually *decide to do it*. First of all, we trust him, rely on him, and count on him being the Anointed One, the Christ. We intend to obey the example and teachings of Jesus. This is the form that *trust* in him takes.

Trusting Christ does not take the form of merely believing certain things about him. Moreover, knowing the "right answers" does not mean we *truly believe* them. To *believe* them means that we are set to *act* as if these "right answers" are true. Perhaps the hardest thing for sincere Christians to come to grips with is the level of real unbelief in their own lives: the unformulated skepticism about Jesus that permeates all dimensions of their being and undermines the efforts they do make toward Christlikeness.

Projects of personal transformation rarely succeed by accident, drift, or imposition. It is choice that matters. Imagine a person wondering day after day if he is/she is going to learn Arabic or if they are going to get married to a certain person—just waiting to see whether it would happen. That would be laughable. But many people live this way with respect to their spiritual transformation.

A certain fatalism in our culture convinces us that inner change is not likely to occur. We say such things as, "That's just the way I am." We even urge ourselves and others to accept this and be done with it. Perhaps we do this in place of beating ourselves up, which is a destructive habit many Christians have.

But recognizing and accepting one's current condition is only a place to start—a valuable preliminary step. There is hope! Now that I see who I really am—lazy, moody, or pretentious—what am I to do next? What is the way forward? These are questions we ask of God and perhaps also of a friend or spiritual director. God will surely give us direction—small, ingenious ideas that will change us on the inside.

⟟ TODAY'S EXPERIMENT ⟟

Reflect upon what has perhaps blocked your intentions toward spiritual formation:

- You don't have an adequate vision of life in God's kingdom.
- You haven't seriously examined what Jesus said and did, so that you can attempt those things.
- You don't trust Jesus, rely on him, and count on him being the Anointed One, the Christ (even though you may have made an initial decision to do so).
- You think that knowing the right doctrine is enough.
- You have doubts about who Jesus was when he walked on earth and if he behaved wisely and with God's hand upon him (although you wouldn't say this to anyone at church).
- You have accepted that living life by accident or drift is normal

and that those who make choices and live intentionally aren't "fun."

- You have spent so much time learning to accept yourself as you are that you haven't asked what the way forward might be.

If any of these possibilities are true about you, what would your next steps be in addressing them?

CHAPTER

20

VIM: MEANS

The vision and solid intention to obey Christ will naturally lead us to seek out and apply the means to that end. We have rich resources for these means in the example and teachings of Jesus, in the Scriptures, and in his people. Through such means, the inner character of the "lost" person is replaced with the inner character of Jesus: his vision, understanding, feelings, decisions, and character.

When my neighbor who has triumphed over me in the past now stands before me with a need I can remedy, I will not be able to do the good thing on the spot if my inner being is filled with thoughts, feelings, and habits that characterize the ruined soul. If I intend to obey Jesus Christ, I must find the means of changing my inner being until it is substantially like his, pervasively characterized by his thoughts, feelings, habits, and relationship with the Father.

When not on the spot, I can retrain my thinking by *study* and *meditation* on Christ himself and on the teachings in Scripture about God, his world, and my life—especially the teachings of Jesus in the Gospels, further elaborated by an understanding of the remainder of the Bible. I can help my thinking and my feelings by deep *reflection* on the nature and bitter outcome of the standard human way in such situations in contrast to the way of Jesus. I can consciously practice explicitly *self-sacrificial actions* in other less demanding situations. I can become a person for whom looking out for number one is not the framework of life.

I can *learn about* and *meditate* upon the lives of well-known saints who have practiced continuously in real life Jesus' way with adversaries and those in need. I can earnestly and repeatedly *pray* that God will directly work in my inner being to change the things there that will enable me to obey his Son. And many other things can be done as a means to fulfilling the vision of life in God that I intend and have chosen.

As we become more and more enthralled by the vision of the kingdom of God, it follows that we want to be shaped by God and so live life more intentionally. We start making small plans and taking tentative steps for this change. With God's grace drawing us along, we arrange our lives differently. We give up certain activities because we want time to do things we're reasonably sure will help reshape us. Here and there, we give up a shopping trip, doing without an item we thought we needed (*frugality*), because we'd rather reread a book that really spoke to us (*study* and *meditation*). We intentionally take stationery with us to the doctor's office so that as we sit in the waiting room we can jot a note to our friend's son who is in jail, instead of reading whatever magazines happen to be there (*service*). We make a little effort to arrive at church early to greet that stranger who's been sitting alone at the back of the sanctuary (*welcoming strangers*). We aren't heroic about these things, and we don't turn them into chores, but we take seriously the ideas for disciplines that come to us that are most likely the prodding of the Holy Spirit. As the means help us, our vision and intention become stronger yet.

✎ TODAY'S EXPERIMENT ✎

What disciplines, if any, do you find yourself drawn to? Consider small practices of solitude, silence, prayer, meditation, study, confession, reflection, service, secrecy, frugality, fasting, community, worship, and celebration.

How might practicing some of these disciplines enhance your vision of the kingdom of God? Perhaps you found value in reading those gospel chapters mentioned a few devotions ago and would like to do that on a regular basis (*study* and *meditation*). Perhaps there are people you know whose lives resemble the teaching and character of Jesus and you would like to serve alongside them in a project they're involved in (*service* and *community*). Perhaps reading this book is helping you see that you need to spend a morning in *solitude, practicing the presence of God* and *confessing* what has come to you in the reading. Perhaps you would like to *pray* for a neighbor who has triumphed over you so that the next time you're on the spot with that person, you can behave with love and concern. Ask God to show you what is next.

21

OUR FIRST FREEDOM

The *ultimate freedom we have as human beings is the power to select what we will allow our mind to dwell upon.* There the light of God first moves upon us through the Word of Christ, and there the Divine Spirit begins to direct our will to thoughts that help us realign ourselves with God and his way.

By thoughts we mean memories, perceptions, and beliefs, as well as what we would ordinarily refer to when we say, "I thought of you yesterday." When we constantly and thoughtfully engage ourselves with the ideas, images, and information that are provided by God through the Scriptures, his Son Jesus, and the lives and experiences of his people through the ages, we are nourished by the Holy Spirit in ways far beyond our own efforts or understanding. This transforms our entire life. All that enters our mind, and especially the thoughts that first come to mind as we encounter people and events, will be healthy, godly, and good. The conclusions we jump to will be those in harmony with the realities of a good, God-governed universe, not the illusions of a godless or a me-governed universe. Our patterns of thinking will conform to the truths of scriptural revelation, and we will apply those truths under the guidance of God's Holy Spirit to all of the details of our daily lives.

Are we undertaking some task? Then in faith we do it *with God*, assuming and finding his power to be involved with us. Is there an emergency? We meet it with the knowledge that God is in the midst of it *with us*, and we are calm in a center of intense prayer. Are we praised? Our thoughts (and feelings) move immediately to the goodness of God in our lives. Are we condemned or reproached? We know that God supports and helps us because he loves us and has a future for us. Are we disappointed and frustrated? We rest in the knowledge that God is over all and that he is working things out. Spiritual transformation of our thought life is achieved by the ministry of the Spirit in the midst of our necessary and well-directed efforts.

The idea that *our first freedom is where we put our mind* is a fundamental one that can guide our lives. For example, I was ruled by self-pity for many years and saw myself as the victim of others. The change in my thinking occurred as I began putting my mind elsewhere—on God as an abiding presence in my life, conscious that just maybe the Lord really is my Shepherd today and I just might have everything I need.

When I understand that my first freedom is where I place my mind, I examine what I've been dwelling on the last few minutes. Regarding a certain person, what thoughts have I had about him or her? I have alternatives now. I can change my thoughts and bless that person, especially if he or she is difficult for me in some way. I can focus my mind on praying for that person. I can ask God to guide me in some way to help that person.

This idea also makes use of the VIM pattern. Where I put my mind creates my vision for the circumstances or persons in front of me. My intentions (attitude) and means (words of conversation, deeds of ignoring or caring) then flow from my vision.

⁓ TODAY'S EXPERIMENT ⁓

Try moving through the next few hours with this idea in front of you: *The first freedom is where I put my mind.* Observe where you have put your mind. If you have not noticed the goodness of God in the blessings around you or found confidence in ideas like those found in Psalm 23, don't make a big deal out of evaluating yourself. Instead, pray for the person or circumstances in front of your eyes at that moment. How might you will God's goodness? Keep moving forward, alert to God's goodness and asking God questions for guidance.

IDEAS: FROM DARK TO LIGHT

Two of the most powerful facets in the realm of thought are *ideas* and *images*. Ideas are ways of thinking about and interpreting things. They are so essential to how we approach life that we often do not understand when and how ideas are at work. Our idea system grows up with us from childhood out of the teachings, expectations, and behaviors of family and community. People are often so far in the grip of ideas that they can't be bothered to think. They don't know what moves them, but ideas govern them and have their consequences anyway.

Examples of ideas are freedom, education, happiness, "the American Dream," the feminine or masculine, and so on. To see ideas in action, look closely at artistic endeavors, especially movies and music, which encapsulate most of pop culture, and at efforts to persuade, especially politics and commercials. Look, for example, at the place *freedom*, a major idea now, plays in automobile ads and rock lyrics.

One task of spiritual formation is to have our ideas transformed. By the Spirit, we replace in ourselves those idea systems of evil with the idea system that Jesus Christ embodied and taught.

The apostle Paul warned that "our struggle is not against flesh and blood, but against the rulers, against the powers, against the world forces of this darkness, against the spiritual forces of wickedness in the heavenly places" (Ephesians 6:12). These powers and forces are spiritual agencies that work with the idea systems of evil. These systems are the powers' *main tool* for dominating humanity.

Changing those governing ideas is one of the most difficult and painful things in life. Such change rarely happens to the individual or group except in the form of divine intervention, revolution, or something like a mental breakdown. Jesus confronted and undermined an idea system and its culture, which in turn killed him. He proved himself greater than any idea system or culture, and he lives on. He is continuing the process of a worldwide idea shift that is crucial to *his* perpetual revolution, in which we each are assigned a part.

When I do something to impress others, I reveal that I live out of a core set of *ideas* that I believe will advance my reputation if I pursue them. These ideas may spring from my personal longings or those established by society—governing ideas highly regarded by family, friends, strangers I meet at retreats or speaking engagements, and the culture at large. But in my pursuit of these ideas (such as the appearance of being in control), I am not trusting that the Lord is my Shepherd and that God provides everything I need—including the reputation I deserve. From a kingdom perspective, the ideas I've adopted—powerful as they may be—are deceptions.

Our versions of these ideas are often a mystery to us and may have little to do with what we profess to believe. We're not being deceitful—we simply don't realize what our core ideas are. One way to discover them is to look backward at one of our behaviors, choices, or responses to someone and ask, What does this tell me about what I believe in the depths of myself?

For example, we embrace ideas about happiness such as, *I must do whatever it takes to be happy*, or ideas about contempt such as, *Labeling and name-calling are acceptable if I am right and the other person is wrong*.

We hold dear certain core ideas about ourselves that govern everything about us:

- *No one will love me if they know what I am really like.*
- *I must work harder to prove myself.*
- *Eating more, spending more, or being sexier will meet my needs or make me feel better about myself.*

❧ Today's Experiment ❧

Engage in some exploratory, listening prayer about your core ideas. Begin by acknowledging to God that you want the mind of Christ to be in you and ask God to renew your mind (see Romans 12:2).

Then ask God to help you with your first step of discerning what core ideas now govern your thinking. Jot down what comes to mind so you can refine them later, returning to them as you are able. If you wish, go over a recent situation in which you behaved in a way that makes you now feel uncomfortable. What core ideas dictated your behavior? Don't be afraid to be brutally honest. God is not surprised by any of this and longs to process it all with you.

Close by asking God to show you your next steps, perhaps asking, What ideas am I to embrace instead? What corrective thinking do I need? If you're unsure, consult a wise friend.

IMAGES: IDEAS PICTURED

Closely associated with governing ideas are *images*, which are concrete or specific as opposed to the abstractness of ideas. They are laden with feeling. In recent history, hair (long, short, skinhead, green, orange, purple) has provided powerful images of conflicting idea systems. In many churches today, the services have divided into traditional and contemporary, so that the guitar and pipe organ are no longer just musical instruments but powerful symbols. Such divisions are not unimportant or sinful, but one does have to understand *what drives such divisions* in order to act responsibly in relation to them.

Jesus carefully selected an image that conveys himself and his message: the cross. It presents the lostness of humans as well as the sacrifice of God and the abandonment to God that brings redemption. No doubt it is the all-time most powerful image and symbol of human history.

Ideas and images can be a stronghold of evil in the human self and society. They determine how we understand the things and events of ordinary life, and they can even blind us to what lies plainly before us. Ideas and images are the primary focus of Satan's efforts to defeat God's purposes with and for humankind. When we are subject to Satan's ideas and images, he can take a holiday. Thus, when he undertook to draw Eve away from God, he did not hit her with a stick, but with an idea: that God could not be trusted and that she must act on her own to secure her own well-being. The single most important thing in our mind is our idea of God and the images associated with it.

Images increase the danger of inadequate ideas. They have the power to obsess and to hypnotize, as well as to escape critical scrutiny.

To *manipulate* images—and thereby people—is the work of the propagandist and the advertiser. Unfortunately, it is often done in the name of Christ to achieve some desired result. The process of spiritual formation in Christ is one of *progressively* replacing those destructive images and ideas with the images and ideas that filled the mind of Jesus himself. We thereby come increasingly to see "the light of the gospel of the glory of Christ, who is the image of God" (2 Corinthians 4:4, NRSV).

Carefully placed images persuade us to forgo thinking and accept ideas we might normally question. For example, putting the flag of one's country on a product or event aims to brand it as good and wholesome when it may not be. Images that seem benign in movies may also "teach" an idea that, if we thought about it, would appall us. But we unthinkingly accept the idea because we like the image.

ᴥ TODAY'S EXPERIMENT ᴪ

Consider your images of God. While Scripture puts forth images such as breath and wind and fire and cloud, be honest with yourself: What really comes to mind when you think of God? For many, God is a benevolent giant who is too busy for them, a clever boss who pulls the rug out from under them just when they thought they knew what was going on, or a hard-nosed teacher who demands much of them.

Give some thought to what ideas drive your images of God. What do you routinely think about God (even though you might never tell anyone at church)? Finish this sentence: God is the kind of being who . . .

Pause and pray. Ask God to show you your true images of him.

Once you have recognized them, consider some new images that represent the true love and goodness of God: one who sings over you, quieting you with love (see Zephaniah 3:17); one who shelters you from chaos under his wings or hidden in a strong tower (see Psalm 91:4; Proverbs 18:10); a jilted lover who keeps wooing you and calling, "Return to me" (see Jeremiah 3:6-10); a column of fire guiding you, continually moving in front of you (see Exodus 13:21-22). Consider choosing an image of God to put at the front of your mind as soon as you wake up in the morning or as you drift to sleep at night.

24

INFORMATION AND
THE ABILITY TO THINK

Two other factors in our thought life can be used by God to break the power of the toxic system of ideas and images that make us dead to God. These are *information* (or facts) and *our ability to think* — to connect things in our mind. After God has implanted new life from above in us by Word and Spirit, we must take the initiative in progressively *retaking the whole of our thought life for God's kingdom*.

Failure to know what God is really like and what his law requires destroys the soul, ruins society, and leaves people to eternal ruin: "My people are destroyed for lack of knowledge," and "A people without understanding comes to ruin" (Hosea 4:6,14, NRSV). This is the tragic condition of Western culture today, which has put away the information about God that God himself has made available.

Spiritual formation requires thinking. The gospel of Jesus repudiates false information about God and the meaning of human life, and it works to undermine the power of those ideas and images that structure life away from God. But for it to have this effect we must *use* our ability to think.

What is thinking? It is the activity of searching out what *must* be true or *cannot* be true in the light of given facts or assumptions. It extends the information we have and enables us to see the larger picture clearly. It undermines false or misleading ideas and images. It is a powerful gift from God to be used in the service of truth.

We must apply our thinking to the Word of God. We must thoughtfully take it in, dwell upon it, ponder its meaning, and explore its implications, especially as it relates to our own lives. We must *seek the Lord* by devoting our powers of thinking to understanding the facts and information of the gospel. This is the primary way of focusing our mind on him, setting him before us.

To read certain verses to fulfill a Bible reading system is not to take the Scripture in, to dwell upon it, to ponder its meaning and to explore its implications. Often, it's an effort to perform, to check off one more thing I need to do today to be a decent Christian. This explains why many folks know a lot of Bible trivia but do not meet God when they open the Scripture. To dwell, to ponder, to explore means reading slowly and wondering what life, reality, or even I personally would look like if this passage were *really* true. It means asking, What is God saying to me today?

ᨏ Today's Experiment ᨏ

Read the following slowly: "Since, then, you have been raised with Christ, set your hearts on things above, where Christ is seated at the right hand of God. Set your minds on things above, not on earthly things. For you died, and your life is now hidden with Christ in God. When Christ, who is your life, appears, then you also will appear with him in glory" (Colossians 3:1-4, NIV).

Ask the Holy Spirit to guide you as you ponder *one* of these questions (whichever one grabs you) and read the passage again:

- What would it look like to *set my heart* (will, spirit) on things above? What things above?
- What would it look like to *set my mind* (ideas, images, information) on things above? What things above?
- What in the world does being "hidden with Christ in God" mean? Why might that be something I would want?
- "Appears" is also translated "is revealed" (NRSV). Consider what Christ being revealed in (or to you in) your daily life would mean about your spiritual formation.

After you have dwelt upon, pondered, and explored the verses and a question above, respond to God. Try writing a prayer or saying it aloud to make it more relational and give it concreteness.

25

CRUCIAL ROLE
OF GOOD THINKING

The prospering of God's cause on earth depends upon his people thinking well. Today we are apt to downplay the importance of good thinking in favor of strong faith, and some, disastrously, even regard thinking as opposed to faith. They do not realize that in so doing they are not honoring God but simply yielding to the deeply anti-intellectualist currents of Western egalitarianism, rooted, in turn, in the romantic idealization of impulse and blind *feeling* found in Hume, Rousseau, and their nineteenth- and twentieth-century followers. They do not realize that they are operating on the same satanic principle that produced the killing fields of Cambodia, where those with any sign of education, even the wearing of glasses, were killed on the spot or condemned to starvation and murderous labor. Bluntly, to serve God well we must think straight. Crooked thinking, unintentional or not, always favors evil.

To take the information of the Scripture into a mind thinking straight under the direction and empowerment of the Holy Spirit is to place our feet solidly on the high road of spiritual formation under God. The psalmist told us,

> The law of the LORD is perfect, restoring the soul;
> The testimony of the LORD is sure, making wise the simple. . . .
> The commandment of the LORD is pure, enlightening the eyes.
> (19:7-8)

To bring the mind to dwell intelligently upon God as presented in his Word will cause us to love God passionately, and this love will bring us to think of God steadily. Thus God will always be before our mind.

In this way we enter a *life of worship*. To think of God as he is, one cannot but lapse into worship, and worship is the single most powerful force in completing and sustaining restoration in the whole person. It puts into abeyance every evil tendency in every dimension of the self. It naturally arises from thinking rightly of God on the basis of revealed truth confirmed in experience. *Worship is at once the overall character of the renovated thought life and the only safe place for a human being to stand.*

Some people's understanding of God keeps growing; their vision of the kingdom of God becomes increasingly richer. They don't mind being stretched and having to think things through.

We can become Spirit-oriented thinkers if we ask the Spirit to help us as we approach Scripture or even the newspaper opinion page or a magazine that stretches us. We can seek guidance, asking, How does this square with what I already know or think? Is my thinking straight here? Is there something here I need to learn?

You can always tell such truth-seekers because they connect the dots between two things that seem to be opposites. They see what others miss, such as in the above text in which Dallas links a thoughtful, studious approach to life with worship of God. Many people concentrate only on worship or only on study to the exclusion of the other. In contrast, study and worship should flow together. Students of God remain humble when they worship, and worshippers who also study worship with substance and truth instead of sentimentality.

⌘ TODAY'S EXPERIMENT ⌘

For five to ten minutes, read something that stretches you or differs from what you might normally think: Scripture (try an Old Testament prophet), your newspaper's opinion page (read a viewpoint opposite your own), a magazine that challenges you (perhaps *Atlantic Monthly* or *Discover*). Pray before you read it, asking the Holy Spirit to help you read slowly and thoughtfully. Pause frequently and ask yourself how this information compares or contrasts with your usual point of view.

Pause afterward. Consider if your reading brings to mind *anything* you might worship God for: the creativity of human relationships, God's truth compared to the false reality routinely presented, or something else.

26

GOD'S THOUGHTS *IN* YOU

Nourishing our mind with good and godly ideas, images, information, and the ability to think creates our *vision* (recall the VIM structure). From these, we *intend* to be formed so that God is a constant presence in our mind, crowding out false ideas, destructive images, misinformation about God, and crooked beliefs. As for *means*, certain tried and true disciplines aid us in the transformation of our thought life toward the mind of Christ. We cannot transform our ideas, images, information, or thought processes into Christlikeness by direct effort, but we can adopt certain practices that indirectly will have that effect.

The most obvious thing we can do is draw certain key portions of Scripture into our mind and make them a part of the permanent fixtures of thought. This is the primary discipline for the thought life. We need to know these passages like the back of our hand, and a good way to do that is to memorize them and then *constantly turn them over* in our mind as we go through the events and circumstances of our lives (see Joshua 1:8; Psalm 1).

The desired effect will not be realized by focusing on isolated verses but will come as we ingest *passages* such as Romans 5:1-8 or 8:1-15, 1 Corinthians 13, or Colossians 3:1-17. When we take these into our mind, our mind will become filled with the light of God himself.

You might say, "I can't memorize like that." I assure you, you certainly can. God made your mind for it, and he will help you. He *really* wants you to do this. As you choose to give your time and energy to the renovation of your mind (*intend* it), *it will happen!*

I gave up memorizing Scripture years ago because I'd made it into a legalism. I worked hard at getting every word right, but I never turned it over in my mind.

But then certain passages became near and dear to me, and I couldn't resist. I'd studied their structure and how they fit together. I'd meditated on them and *entered into* them. Certain phrases rolled off my tongue with fondness. Without realizing it, I'd engaged in the three keys to memorizing that Dallas mentions elsewhere: repetition, concentration (focus), and understanding.

Finally, I decided to embrace Colossians 3:1-17 because it pictured who I wanted to be. So on a lark, as I sat in an almost empty shuttle bus for a thirty-minute ride, I faced the window and began memorizing it. It began making even more sense to me! I noted phrases that still puzzled me so I could study them further. It was as if my mind finally gave in to my heart, which loved the ideas expressed in this passage and wanted them to be a description of who I was becoming.

⤙ TODAY'S EXPERIMENT ⤚

Please resist skipping this experiment. A passage of Scripture that is relatively easy to memorize is 1 Corinthians 13. If you've been to a few weddings, you've almost got it. Once you know it, you can enjoy it as a description of God (patient, kind) and of life in the kingdom (seeing dimly now, face-to-face soon!) while you're doing yard work or waiting in line at a store.

Before trying to memorize it, however, read it slowly—maybe every day for a week or several times a day. Print it out and carry it around with you. Relish the words and ideas. See how they fit together. Notice progressions. Picture the people you know who embody these verses. Picture God's love for you. Get so familiar with the passage that it would be difficult *not* to memorize it.

Perhaps you could give just verses 4-7 a try. They begin with two "is" statements: patient and kind. These are followed by six "does not/is not" statements: envy, boast, proud, rude, self-seeking, easily angered. These six flow back and forth from inward (envy, proud, self-seeking) to outward (boast, rude, easily angered). They're all about self-preoccupation. Then come the two more complicated phrases: no record of wrongs, not delighting in evil but rejoicing in truth. Then the passage ends with the four "always" phrases (first and last begin with *p*): protects, trusts, hopes, perseveres. This last set has become a quick prayer for me when I'm in a business meeting and want to strangle someone. I pray that I may always protect, always trust, always hope, always persevere.

27

MASTERED BY FEELINGS

Feelings live in the front row of our lives like unruly children clamoring for attention. No one can succeed in mastering feelings who tries to take them head-on and resist or redirect them by willpower in the moment of choice.

Those who continue to be mastered by their feelings—such as anger, fear, sexual attraction, desire for food, need for looking good, or the residues of woundedness—are typically persons who in their heart of hearts believe that their *feelings must be satisfied*. They have long chosen the strategy of *resisting* their feelings instead of *changing* or *replacing* them. This creates a ruined person who makes himself "god" in his world. By contrast, the person who happily lets God be God accepts that feelings do *not* have to be fulfilled.

Achieving this new vision of oneself requires openness to radical change, careful instruction, and abundant supplies of divine grace. For most people this comes only after they hit bottom and discover the hopelessness of their path. They cannot envision who they would be without the fears, angers, lusts, power ploys, and woundedness they learned in the home, school, and playground. But with this new vision, they now see themselves as ones being transformed to characterize the inner being of Jesus Christ. Now they can stop being persons who spend hours fantasizing sensual indulgence or revenge or who try to dominate or injure others in attitude, word, or deed. Now they will not repay evil for evil—push for push, blow for blow, taunt for taunt, contempt for contempt. They will not be always on the hunt to satisfy their lust of the flesh, lust of the eyes, and pride of life (see 1 John 2:16).

At first such persons have no idea who they will be if they "put off the old person" (involving the wrong feeling) and "put on the new person" (involving the good feeling). To long for the identity of a mere "apprentice of Jesus" is the starting point from which a new identity emerges.

How would you finish this sentence: Who would I be if I weren't_____ _____? Perhaps you might say moody, passionate (often a euphemism for opinionated), particular (as in a perfectionist), or funny (which may take the form of a merciless tease or a sarcastic wit). We've known ourselves to be a certain way for so long. We've heard people say, "She's just that way," and it has become part of our identity. One man I knew didn't feel really alive unless he was in a rage.

⁓ TODAY'S EXPERIMENT ⁓

Picture an imaginary conversation with someone who knows you well. Ask this person what he or she would change about you if it were possible. Then put yourself in the presence of God and read these verses to God:

> Put to death, therefore, whatever belongs to your earthly nature: sexual immorality, impurity, lust, evil desires and greed, which is idolatry. Because of these, the wrath of God is coming. You used to walk in these ways, in the life you once lived. But now you must rid yourselves of all such things as these: anger, rage, malice, slander, and filthy language from your lips. Do not lie to each other, since you have taken off your old self with its practices and have put on the new self, which is being renewed in knowledge in the image of its Creator. (Colossians 3:5-10, NIV)

Pray, asking God one of these questions: Is it really possible to . . .

- put to death whatever belongs to my earthly nature?
- take off my old self with its practices?
- put on a new self, which is being *renewed in knowledge in the image of my Creator*?

If you wish, continue going over that last phrase, asking God to give you a glimpse of what it would look like to be renewed in knowledge in the image of your Creator. This is part of what God wants for you.

28

HIDDEN DYNAMICS OF FEELINGS

Many of the feelings that animate us are destructive to others and ourselves. James pointedly asked, "What is the source of quarrels and conflicts among you? Is not the source your pleasures that wage war in your members? You lust and do not have; so you commit murder. You are envious and cannot obtain; so you fight and quarrel. . . . Where jealousy and selfish ambition exist, there is disorder and every evil thing" (4:1-2; 3:16). This explains what happens in many homes and churches. The need is not just to remove the conflict but also to address underlying feelings.

The *underlying* feelings are settled *conditions* that lie beneath feelings. For example, one can live in the *underlying condition* of hatred, contempt, hurry, or discouragement but not always have the accompanying feelings. We've managed the feelings, but we still live in that condition. (Or on the positive side, one can live with the underlying condition of peace but may or may not always have feelings of peacefulness.) Those negative underlying conditions of our character must be addressed.

Feelings can creep into other areas of our lives, changing the overall tone. They may take over our entire being and so determine the outcome of our lives as a whole. This explains why it is hard to reason with some people. Their mind has been *taken over* by certain feelings and serves those feelings *at all costs*. Some people never escape this fearful condition.

Feelings can be successfully "reasoned with" and corrected by reality only in those who have the habit and are given the grace of *listening* to reason even when they are expressing violent feelings or are in the grip of them. Otherwise, strong feelings may blot out all else for those who have not been trained to identify, be critical of, and have some *distance from their own feelings*. A wise person will carefully keep the pathway open to the house of reason and go there regularly to listen.

We may congratulate ourselves for sailing through a disturbing experience without "shooting our mouth off" but overlook the fact that we were primed to do so because of our underlying condition of contempt for certain people or certain situations. In our mind, we concluded that this person didn't really know what he was talking about—compared to us! We may have kept our arrogance and know-it-all attitude quiet, but anything could have happened. (And our attitude may have "leaked out" anyway in our body language.) These settled conditions that underlie our feelings don't seem wrong because we've developed culturally acceptable, euphemistic ways to disguise them: I'm not exacting, just careful!

Because having a settled attitude (underlying condition) of contempt is common today, it's important to listen carefully to our thought patterns regarding certain people and observe how we speak to and about them. We need to pay special attention not only to the background noise in our head but also to our tone of voice (so revealing), to the hunch of our shoulders, and to the set of our lips. These can be telling symptoms of our underlying attitudes.

❧ TODAY'S EXPERIMENT ❧

Reflect on what might be a common underlying condition for you, such as hurry or discouragement or contempt. Try to put some distance between yourself and the condition in order to examine it. When did it start? Why are you now convinced you must hurry (or live in discouragement or look down on others)? What underlying condition is God inviting you to adopt instead? Consider how it would make your life lighter and easier (see Matthew 11:30).

THE POWER OF THE "MOOD"

In modern times, *feelings* exercise almost total mastery over the individual. When people must decide what they want to do, feelings are all they have to go on. This is why contemporary Western life is peculiarly prone to gross immoralities and addictions. *People are overwhelmed with decisions and can make those decisions only on the basis of feelings.*

As a result, people cannot distinguish between their feelings and their will, and they confuse feelings with reasons. They lack self-control, which is the steady capacity to direct yourself to accomplish what you have chosen or decided to do and be, even though you "don't feel like it." Without self-control, people drift through the days and years using addictive behavior to endure.

Ideas and images foster and sustain feelings. Hopelessness and rejection live on images—often of a specific scene of unkindness, brutality, or abuse—that have become permanent fixtures within our mind, radiating negativity and leaving a background of deadly ideas that take over how we think. Such images cultivate moods, which *pervade* our selves and everything around us.

Denial and repression of destructive feelings are not the answer. But feelings can be transformed by discipleship to Christ and the power of the gospel and the Spirit, through which the corresponding ideas and images are changed to positive ones. The proper course of action is to *replace* destructive feelings with others that are good or to *subordinate* them—anger and sexual desire, for example—in a way that makes them constructive. We do not *try first to root out these destructive feelings, but they are eliminated as we make the first move:* going toward love, joy, and peace, based on faith and hope in God.

Then we experience feelings and moods associated with confidence, being acceptable, belonging, purposefulness, love, hope, joy, and peace. Being "accepted in the beloved" (Ephesians 1:6, KJV) is the humanly indispensable foundation for the reconstruction of all these positive feelings, moods, and their underlying conditions.

If it feels as though our feelings are bigger than we are (like a giant boogeyman hunching over us), it's because they're being fed by the ideas and images we cultivate, especially those we play over in our mind. Because my first freedom is where I put my mind, I can ask, What ideas and images am I giving airtime to?

For example, I grew up as a lazy child, and now I sometimes struggle to get myself seated at my desk. Although I faithfully show up for work, I despair over these feelings of laziness. What ideas and images might contribute to this? One of several is that I live in a culture that does not value work but instead tries to get out of it. Most people I know would love to win the lottery and retire immediately. But when work is valued, it's as a means to productivity, achievement, and good reputation. I have somehow bought into the idea that work is bad and I should be able to get out of it. On the other hand, I love my work. Once I get going, I never want to quit. How confusing!

A replacement image that helps me is that of several older friends who genuinely love to work hard and be useful. They work fruitfully and cheerfully and often produce things of great beauty—a new barn door or an enchanting dessert.

❧ TODAY'S EXPERIMENT ❧

Consider a feeling that plagues you—one you wish you didn't have. Set aside a time to ponder this before God, perhaps writing about it in a journal. Ask God to reveal to you the ideas and images you have (perhaps unknowingly) chosen to maintain. Sit quietly and ask God what feelings might replace these (perhaps love, joy, peace, confidence, or hope). Finally, consider what ideas and images would foster that replacement feeling.

FEELINGS OF THE SPIRITUALLY TRANSFORMED PERSON

What feelings will dominate a life that has been inwardly transformed to be like Christ's? They are feelings associated with love, joy, peace, and their underlying conditions. Also, faith (confidence) and hope are important in properly structuring the feeling dimension of the mind and self.

Hope is anticipation of "unseen" *good* not yet here. Sometimes the good is deliverance from present evil, so we "rejoice in hope" (Romans 12:12, PAR). Closely related to hope, faith is confidence grounded in reality—not a wild, desperate "leap." Faith sees the reality of the unseen, and it includes a readiness to act as if the anticipated good were already in hand because of the reality of God (compare 2 Corinthians 4:17-18).

Faith and hope in Christ lead us to stand in the grace (the action) of God, which leads to a life full of love. *Love* is will-to-good. We love others when we promote their good. We wish them well. Love's contrary is malice, and its simple absence is indifference. Love is not the same as *desire*, for I may desire something without even wishing it well. I might desire chocolate ice cream, but I do not wish it well. I wish to eat it. This is the difference between lust (mere desire) and love. Desire and love are compatible when desire is ruled by love, but many people today do not know the difference between them. Hence, love constantly falls prey to lust. That is a major part of the deep sickness of contemporary life.

Pride and *fear* no longer rule our lives when love is primary. Pride is defined by desire. It presumes that my desires should be fulfilled and that it is a crying shame if they are not. Lust and pride inevitably result in fear, for they bring us into a world of little dictators where people use and abuse others instead of helping and caring for them. The opposite of love is pride. Love eliminates pride because it nullifies our arrogant presumption that we should get *our* way. With love, pride and fear fade.

Sometimes faith, hope, and love seem so lofty that they must be beyond an ordinary person such as me. At that point, it helps to picture some of the people in Scripture as if they were folks next door. At eighty-plus years old (will I even *live* that long?), Moses "left Egypt, not fearing the wrath of the king" (Hebrews 11:27). (How could that be? I fear the IRS.) Moses didn't pay attention to Pharaoh because he was only part of the realm of "the seen." He stuck with his goal of delivering Israel because he saw the One who is invisible but nevertheless real. "For he endured, as seeing Him who is unseen" (11:27).

Because of Moses' hope and confidence in God (most of the time), this stunning, aged leader lived an adventurous, dramatic, and God-infused life without fear. When I picture myself interviewing him, I imagine him saying that the entire Exodus event was so obviously beyond him and in God's power that he felt as if he were simply watching God do it (see Isaiah 63:11-13). No wonder Moses managed to be the most humble person on earth (see Numbers 12:3). He could lead and direct without pride.

Could I live "as seeing Him who is unseen"? I imagine that if Moses heard me say that in the interview, he would probably wink at me and ask, "What if I'd stayed behind in Midian herding sheep? Look what I would have missed!" This picture (*vision*) of Moses inspires me to *intend* to live in confidence and hope and diligently look for the *means*.

❧ Today's Experiment ☙

If you sense that you lack the faith, hope, and love described above, reflect on the life of Moses, a real person (a former murderer hiding out in Midian). Imagine what it would be like to be Moses and genuinely not fear the most powerful person on earth. Imagine what it would be like to live with the hope of a promised land you've never seen but you *know* is real. How would such confidence and hope draw you into a deeper love of God? An overflowing desire to worship God? What would it make you want to say to God?

31

A PERSON OF JOY AND PEACE

Joy is *natural* in the presence of God, whose deepest essence is love. *Joy* is a pervasive sense of well-being that is deeper and broader than any pleasure. It is a basic element of inner transformation into Christlikeness and the outer life that flows from it. Thus Jesus could say to his closest friends on the night before his crucifixion: "These things I have spoken to you so that My joy may be in you, and that your joy may be made full" (John 15:11).

Having your joy "full" is the first line of defense against weakness, failure, and disease of mind and body. But even when they break through into your life, "the joy of the LORD is your strength" (Nehemiah 8:10). We must not be passive and allow joy to dissipate by looking backward at our sins and failures or forward at what might happen to us or inward at our struggles with work, responsibilities, temptations, and deficiencies. In doing this, we place our hopes in the wrong thing, namely ourselves. It is our option to look to the greatness and goodness of God and what he will do in our lives.

Peace is the assurance that things will turn out well. We no longer strive, inwardly or outwardly, to create some outcome. To be at peace with God and others is a great attainment and depends on graces far beyond ourselves and our own efforts.

When others do not extend the grace and mercy I need, I have to draw on the abundance of it in God. "Who is this that is condemning me?" I remind myself, "Jesus even died for me, was raised from the dead, and is now standing up for me before God" (Romans 8:34, PAR). Assurance of this allows me to "pursue peace with all men" (Hebrews 12:14). Even in cases where struggle exists between others and me, there does not have to be a struggle within me. I may have to resist others, but I do not have to make things come out right. I do not have to be mad at those whose course of action I resist.

The secret to this peace, as great apprentices of Jesus have long known, is being abandoned to God. Since God is love and is so great, I live beyond harm in his hands. There is nothing that can happen to me that will not turn out for my good. Nothing. Because of this, "Thou wilt keep him in perfect peace, whose mind is stayed on thee: because he trusteth in thee" (Isaiah 26:3, KJV).

Does it seem odd to you that abandonment to God should be mentioned in the same breath as joy? Isn't abandonment a miserable thing? Maybe abandonment would go with peace, but certainly not joy. How can this be?

Yet once we move below the surface, we see that peace *and joy* are based on confidence in God (faith). In this confidence, I can abandon myself to God, even die to myself. As I do these things, striving will cease and joy will naturally flow. I may even now and then "be anxious for nothing" and experience the peace of God as it *guards* my heart and mind in Christ Jesus (Philippians 4:6-7).

⨳ TODAY'S EXPERIMENT ⨳

As a means of knowing the joy and peace of God, consider praying a few of these prayers of release: "O God, I long for your perfect peace that is beyond my understanding. I now release to you the habit of:

- dwelling on certain past sins and failures, such as . . .
- looking forward at what might happen to me if . . .
- fixing my eyes inward at struggles with work, responsibilities, temptations, and deficiencies, such as . . .
- putting trust in myself to work things out with . . .
- having to make things come out right with . . .
- being mad at . . . whose actions I've had to resist.

"Thou wilt keep me in perfect peace as my mind is stayed on thee, because I trust in thee" (Isaiah 26:3, PAR).

32

NEXT STEPS TOWARD LOVE, JOY, AND PEACE

Renovation of the heart in the dimension of feeling is a matter of opening ourselves up to cultivating love, joy, and peace, first by receiving them from God and those living in him and then by extending them to others. *But we do not approach the change the other way around, trying first to root out the destructive feelings.* That is the common mistake of worldly wisdom. Love, joy, and peace fostered in divine fellowship crowd out fear, anger, unsatisfied desire, woundedness, and rejection. There is no longer room for them—well, perhaps there is for a while, but increasingly less so. Belonging to Christ does not immediately eliminate bad feelings, but it does *crucify* them (see Galatians 5:24). Negative and destructive feelings are on their way to death in those who have put Christ on the throne of their life and have taken their place on his cross.

This is the *vision* in our VIM pattern, but we must also *intend* this in all we are and do. Our thought life will be focused upon God, and so our walk with Jesus will show us the details of the *means* required to bring it to pass.

For many of us, coming to honest terms with our real feelings will be a huge task. To "let love be without hypocrisy" requires serious effort (Romans 12:9). Ordinary life is so permeated with insincere expressions of love, alongside contempt and anger, that it is hard not to feel forced into hypocrisy in some situations. As we learn to avoid it, we shall begin to see what a huge difference that alone makes.

As we recognize the reality of our feelings, we agree with the Lord to abandon those that are destructive and that lead us into doing or being what we know to be wrong. We may need to *write out* what those feelings are in a letter to the Lord or confer about them with a wise Christian friend who knows how to listen to us and God at the same time. The Lord will help us with this.

As we receive love, joy, and peace from God and people and then practice extending them to others, our destructive feelings will become apparent. When they do, it won't help to deny them or to dwell on them. Neither pretending to have joy nor berating ourselves for not having it will help. Instead, we identify destructive feelings and abandon them and then go back to drenching ourselves further in God's love, joy, and peace and passing them on to others by God's empowering grace.

◔ TODAY'S EXPERIMENT ◕

Think about the possible images, ideas, and information of God's love, joy, and peace that resonate with you. They might include something as simple as a hummingbird or as deep as the concept of atonement. Jot down some words or phrases that come to mind.

In the midst of this, consider *destructive feelings* that have come up in you in the last week—perhaps fear, anger, unsatisfied desire, woundedness, or rejection. Don't hurry. (If nothing comes to you, ask God to show you these things as you are adequately prepared to receive them.)

Ask the Spirit to reveal the *underlying settled conditions* that keep these destructive feelings active (vengeance, contempt, self-pity, discouragement, inadequacy). Also ask the Spirit to reveal to you the ideas, images, or bits of information that nurture these feelings and that you keep in front of your mind (or in front of your eyes through media).

Finally, ask the Spirit to replace destructive conditions and feelings with settled conditions of love, joy, and peace (as well as confidence and hope) that will dwell in you. Consider the thoughts you will need to dwell on to cultivate settled conditions of love, joy, and peace.

Close by thanking God for being the essence of love and for willing your good today.

33

CHANGING THE CHARACTER

Transforming the will (heart, spirit) and character is also the task of spiritual formation. Thoughts and feelings depend on the will (choices), yet the will depends upon the contents of the mind (thoughts, feelings). They are an interlocking whole.

Our *character* is that internal structure of the self that is revealed by our longtime patterns of behavior. From it, our actions automatically arise. Credit reports, résumés, and letters of reference reveal what kinds of thoughts, feelings, and tendencies of will we habitually act from and, therefore, how we will act in the future.

But character can be changed, which is what spiritual formation in Christlikeness is about. If, for example, I have injured someone (possibly a loved one) by speaking or acting in anger, I may be remorseful and ask myself if I really want to be the kind of person who does such things. If I do not want that character, it will be necessary to change my thoughts and feelings. Just resolving not to do it again will be of little use. *Will alone* cannot bring about change. But *will implemented through changing my thoughts and feelings* can result in my becoming the kind of person who doesn't do such things anymore.

In order to change, I must come to possess thoughts and feelings that enable me to choose to change those former thoughts and feelings that caused the anger. By choosing this, I come with "repentance toward God and faith in our Lord Jesus Christ" (Acts 20:21). The human mind and will must be transformed through interaction with thoughts and feelings deriving from the Word and the Spirit.

Now we ask, What does a will or heart look like that has been transformed into Christlikeness? It is characterized by *single-minded and joyous devotion to God and his will, to what God wants for us, and to service to him and to others because of him.* This outcome of Christian spiritual formation becomes our *character* when it governs the responses of every dimension of our being. Then we have "put on Christ" (Galatians 3:27, KJV).

Character is what I feel or do without thinking. I may say, "I didn't mean that," but something in me *did* mean it. My true character "leaks" when I'm not trying to impress anyone or when I don't carefully plot how I should act in order to reflect Christ. When someone cuts me off on the freeway, my true character is reflected by whether I say, "That creep!" or, "Bless you." (Or the intermediate step: "Bless you—you certainly need it!") As we "put on Christ," we love people without trying. Compassion flows.

How jarring Jesus must have been for his disciples. What flowed out of them was so different from what flowed out of Jesus. Consider these contrasts: ignoring kids to move on to important matters/blessing kids as an important matter (Matthew 19:13-15); sending people away to buy their food/checking to see if God had an adventurous idea for feeding them (Matthew 14:15-21); conniving about who will take charge in the future/ simply serving the persons in front of him (Matthew 20:20-28); hurrying to heal an important person's relative/pausing to speak to a woman who had already sneaked her healing from Jesus but needed his listening gaze (Matthew 9:18-22); running off with Greek-speaking Jews to stay out of harm from the Pharisees/staying in Jerusalem and facing death (John 12:20-33). If I'd been one of Jesus' disciples, I would have rolled my eyes at him so many times. This people-focused, purpose-oriented way of life that simply flowed out of him would have baffled me—but intrigued me as well.

TODAY'S EXPERIMENT

Ponder what you admire most about Jesus. (If needed, skim through one of the Gospels and recall the things he did.) What does it show about his character?

Tell Jesus why you admire this quality about him. Ask him to show you what it would look like if this sort of character flowed from you as you decided to let the Trinitarian presence make its home in you (see John 14:23). Ask Jesus to help you become more intentional about having that sort of heart.

34

THE SPLINTERED WILL

Our will is what *comes from nothing else but us*. Will is the ability to originate (or refrain from originating) an act or a thing. It is the core of who and what we are as individuals, for what arises from our will is from us *alone*. It is that aspect of personality that gives us a likeness to God, what we are in his image. The will's primary exercise in humans is the power to select what we think about and how intently we focus on it. From this, our other decisions and actions flow, more or less.

Character develops from will. God doesn't run over our will because it is highly *precious* and gives the person *dignity*. Choice—the *exercise* of will and spirit—is valued and carefully guarded throughout life.

We are created to be creators of good. The drive toward good is naturally implanted in the human will by our Creator, but the will can become splintered, corrupted, and eventually turned against itself as a result of practical self-deification. The question, What good can I bring about? is replaced by How can I get my way? As exaltation of self replaces submission and service to God, manipulation, deception, seduction, and malice replace transparency, sincerity, and goodwill.

Though God reveals his will to us, he chooses *not* to override our self-conflicted will, allowing us the consequences of our choices. Good and wise inclinations are frequently defeated by the flawed inclinations of our lives: social influences, mistaken ideas, overwhelming feelings, or disconnections and ruptures in the depths of the soul.

The constant character of the will apart from God is *duplicity*—or, more accurately, fragmentation and multiplicity. It wills many things, and these cannot be reconciled with each other. Turned away from

God, thoughts and feelings fall into chaos. Then the human will moves irresistibly toward deception. This is the result of pretending to feel and think one way while acting in another. Often the deception involved is self-deception, so that we cannot even understand ourselves and why we do what we do.

One time I was quizzed about how some people supposedly choose Christ but don't choose to be disciples of Jesus. I commented, "And how miserable they are." My questioner was surprised, because playing around with sin isn't miserable, is it?

Yes, it is. You constantly battle with yourself. You fancy some cute man or woman at work but berate yourself for such thoughts. You waffle back and forth wondering if you should or shouldn't help a needy person. You muddle over whether it's so important to get the details exactly right on the tax form. Your life is lived with a foot in two different worlds. This torment is caused by duplicity.

God lets us be miserable because he respects our ability to make choices. If we choose to live a life of fragmented purposes, God does not force us to get our heart right. Yet in the long run, keeping our heart right is much easier. Jesus' yoke really is easier, and his burden is lighter.

❧ TODAY'S EXPERIMENT ❧

Identify the issues you are sick and tired of muddling over: people you wish to control; making more money; acquiring a certain item; having more clout, respect, or admiration. Perhaps you've brooded so long over something that if you relinquished it you would feel as if a part of you died. In a certain sense, that's true. Yet walking through this death to self ("becoming like him in his death") holds the key for participating in a resurrected sort of life with Christ ("to attain to the resurrection from the dead") (Philippians 3:10-11, NIV).

Tell Jesus your fears about such a death to self. Ask him to show you how your life would actually be easier if you just gave up on all these things, how love and joy and peace would be at your right hand.

35

THE VIVID AND ETERNAL DRAMA OF GOD

In the progression toward complete identification of our will with God's, first there is *surrender*. When we surrender our will to God, we consent to his supremacy in all things. We may not be able to do his will, but we are willing to will it. In this condition there is still much grumbling and complaining about our lives and about God.

If grace and wisdom prevail in our surrendered life, we move on to *abandonment*. No part of us holds back from God's will any longer. Typically, at this point, surrender now covers all the circumstances of life. We begin to live in this astonishing reality: Irredeemable harm does not befall those who willingly live in the hand of God.

Beyond abandonment is *contentment* with the will of God, not only with his being who he is and ordaining what he has ordained in general but also with the lot that has fallen to us. At this point, gratitude and joy are the steady tone of our lives. We are now assured that God has done, and will always do, well by us—no matter what! *Dreary, foot-dragging surrender to God looks like a far distant country.* Duplicity looks like utter foolishness in which no sane person would be involved.

Beyond contentment lies intelligent, energetic *participation* in accomplishing God's will in our world. We are no longer spectators but are caught up in a vivid and eternal drama in which we play an essential part. We embrace our imposed circumstances, no matter how tragic they seem, and act for the good in a power beyond ourselves. "We are reigning—exercising dominion—in life by One, Christ Jesus" (Romans 5:17, PAR), looking toward an eternity of reigning with God through ages of ages (see Revelation 22:5).

Our tiny willpower is not the source of our strength. Instead, we are carried along by the power of the divine drama within which we live actively engaged. This is the real meaning of "Yet not I, but Christ liveth in me" (Galatians 2:20, KJV). The strongest human will is always the one that is surrendered to God's will and acts *with* it.

Progressing in this forward movement from surrender to abandonment to contentment to participation is the mysterious secret of wise saints, some of whom you and I may have encountered. (We might consider them to be the people we want to be like "when we grow up.") Believe that you may become one of them. As you do, your life will never, ever be boring because you'll understand that interacting with God creates a daily divine drama that makes the average life in our culture look boring.

⚘ TODAY'S EXPERIMENT ⚘

Consider what it would look like for you to move forward on this continuum of identifying your will with God's: surrender . . . abandonment . . . contentment . . . participation. Ask God for grace and wisdom to help you discern what your next steps could be, including the use of any spiritual disciplines:

- *Confessing* roadblocks
- Practicing *community* with those on this path or those who will stretch you on this path
- *Serving* in a way that makes abandonment a reality
- Practicing *solitude* to surrender yourself regularly

In self-examination processes such as these, we must avoid turning our eyes back on ourselves with recurrent analysis. This is not helpful. Nor is wondering if we'll ever get to *participation*. Such self-preoccupation can, in fact, keep us spinning so that we are not wholly preoccupied with God in our lives. It's better to simply ask God, What do I need to know?

Perhaps what is needed is to simply believe this progression is possible, to believe that you can participate in the divine drama of accomplishing God's will in our world in some way. Here's the reality: Partnering with God in this way on a day-to-day basis can be much more interesting and engaging than any movie you've ever seen.

36

HOW DISCIPLINES HELP

As the will is surrendered, we come to grips with our fallen character, which positions every element of our being against God. We must move out of this entanglement to *single-minded focus* upon doing the will of God in everything, distracted by nothing.

Stepping free of entanglements helps us overcome duplicity. The person who intends to will what God wills begins with what God has *said* he wills. For example, we know it is not God's will to have guile (sneakiness) and malice. Then let us decide today never to mislead people and never to do or say things merely to cause pain or harm. That may sound like a small part of identifying with God's will, but lying and malice are *foundational* sins. They make many other sins possible, including family fights and international warfare.

How do we cause the duplicity and malice that are buried in our will and character to surface and be dealt with? A great help is spiritual disciplines, for example solitude (being alone with God for long periods of time), fasting (learning freedom from food and how God directly nourishes us), worship (adoration of God), and service (doing good for others with no thought of ourselves).

Disciplines make room for the Word and the Spirit to work in us. They permit destructive feelings (veiled by standard excuses and accepted practices) to be perceived and dealt with as our will rather than God's will. Those feelings are normally clothed in layers of self-deception and rationalization. They enslave the will, which coerces the mind to conceal or rationalize what is really going on. Your mind will really "talk to you" when you deny fulfillment of your desires (for example, solitude denies others' company; fasting denies eating).

As we practice solitude or service, we may find that our "righteous judgments" of others are really ways of putting them down and lifting us up. Our extreme busyness may be revealed as inability to trust God or unwillingness to give others a chance to contribute. Our readiness to give our opinions may turn out to be contempt for the thoughts and words of others or simply a willingness to shut them up.

Disciplines create space for the retraining of our thoughts, feelings, and will. We see ourselves as we really are, and the games of duplicity are over.

One of my disciplines of *service* is volunteering at a drop-in center for the homeless. When I began, I had a heart for the homeless. Yet in my times of *solitude*, I saw that I was sometimes rude to clients—stepping in front of them, interrupting them, even talking down to them. So I *confessed* these things. Realizing I needed to learn compassion from Jesus, I began to *study* and *meditate* on gospel passages I'd barely noticed before.

While *serving* there, I learn to *practice the presence of God* as I fold towels and load washers and dryers. I learn to listen to people ramble or complain (*submission*) and *pray* for them. I gain *community* with fellow volunteers who provide me a steady influence of compassion and toughness of purpose. I *celebrate* with God and others many times when someone holds down a job, finds a reasonable apartment, or kicks a habit. I bond with God by weeping over the deaths of clients and the births of drug-addicted babies.

This *service* plays out in a discipline of *secrecy*. Most clients don't know what I do for a living or that I have a "real job." Many people in our middle-class town think our volunteers are wasting their time, as do the Christians in town because the center is not a specifically Christian organization. There's no glory in it—just the wearing of clothes that have been stained by laundry bleach.

Yet this place of *service* has become a place I meet Jesus, who nudges me to love the person in front of me. I can never give as much as I receive there.

❧ Today's Experiment ❧

What sort of discipline has God been nudging you toward: solitude, silence, community, prayer, confession, service, secrecy, frugality, fasting, study, meditation, worship, or celebration? The way God may suggest you practice it might look very different from how someone else practices it. Ask God what he has in mind for your next step.

37

THE BODY'S ROLE
IN SPIRITUAL FORMATION

The body lies at the center of the spiritual life. It is potential energy, and to access that energy is the constant human goal and problem. If there is gasoline in my tank, I can liberate the energy in it and make it do the work of moving my car.

Therefore, my body is the primary place of my dominion and my responsibility. As I proceed in life, first I take dominion over my body itself (eye movement, voice, motion of limbs, and so on). But very quickly I attempt dominion over others, who may have organized their desires contrary to my own. So I experience destructive emotions, especially fear, anger, envy, jealousy, and resentment (example: Cain). These may, in time, develop into settled attitudes of hostility, contempt, or indifference.

Such attitudes make me ready to harm others, and these attitudes quickly settle into my body. There they become more or less overt tendencies to act without thinking in ways that harm others or myself. If left unchecked, they will rule the rest of my life and will constantly inject poison into my social world and personal relations.

Most of what is called *character* (good *or* bad) in normal human life consists in what our bodies are or are not "at the ready" to do in specific situations. These "readinesses" govern our responses and are seen by observant people who then determine how to react to us.

For usual human beings in usual circumstances, their body runs their life. Contrary to the words of Jesus, life is, for them, *not* more than food, nor the body more than clothing (see Matthew 6:25). Their time and energy is almost wholly devoted to how their body looks, smells, and feels, and to how it can be used to meet ego needs such as admiration, sexual gratification, and power over others. That is a perversion of the role of the body in life as God intended it, and it results in "death," in alienation from God and the loss of all we have invested our lives in (see Galatians 6:8).

Who we really are inside is communicated by our manner—what our body is "ready" to do at any minute. The way we stand, the look on our face, the height of our shoulders tells people the condition of our heart. Our body speaks volumes about us.

"The look" is subtle but reveals a great deal. Jesus talks about "looking to lust" (see Matthew 5:28), and a body trained to do so can scarcely not do it. Others steeped in disgust have trained their face to look with disgust, and that is noticed, especially by those younger, less powerful, or somehow subservient on the social ladder.

Sometimes people send mixed signals. They try to "act like a Christian," but their body betrays them. When I'm not around anyone I need to impress, what would it take to get me to yell at someone? What would have to happen for my hand and arm to hit someone?

Today's Experiment

Stand before a full-length mirror. Imagine for a moment you're speaking to someone you dislike. Let your body move into its natural pose for this. Do not mask your true feelings. Examine your body to see if you've arranged it in some way to protect yourself—perhaps your arms are crossed. Notice the position of your eyebrows. Are they raised or lowered? Knitted? Pay attention to how your mouth is set or how your tongue is positioned within your mouth.

Start over. Let's say you are now facing someone from whom you wish a favor. Position yourself. Notice what your eyes, mouth, and arms tell you.

Start again and recall a stressful issue. Look at yourself. Where do you carry your stress? Some bear it in their shoulders, hunching them. Others find their stomachs tightening.

Speak to God about the ways you've trained your body. Admit the underlying settled attitudes that your body favors. If you're confused, ask God, who is "acquainted with all [your] ways" (Psalm 139:3), to help you. God can inform us of these things gently.

38

RETRAINING THE BODY

Spiritual transformation into Christlikeness is the process of forming the inner world of the human self in such a way that it takes on the character of the inner being of Jesus himself. The result is that the "outer" life of the individual increasingly becomes a natural expression of the inner reality of Jesus and his teachings. Doing what he said and did increasingly becomes a part of who we are.

But for this to happen, our body must increasingly be *poised to do* what is good and to refrain from what is evil. The inclinations to wrongdoing that inhabit our body's parts must be eliminated. Then the body becomes a primary ally in Christlikeness.

Without the elimination of such inclinations, the part of our character that lives in our body carries us away. James observed the incredible power of the tongue to stir up the inclinations of the body. It is perhaps the last bodily part to submit to goodness and rightness. No one can tame it. Physical violence is nearly always introduced by verbal violence (see James 3:5-6).

It is only as we habitually subject our tongue to the grace of God as an instrument reserved to do his will that grace comes literally to inhabit and govern it. And when that happens the effects spread throughout the body.

The proper retraining and nurturing of the body is essential to Christlikeness. When our heart (will, spirit) comes to new life in God, the old "programs" still run, primarily *in* our body. "Sin dwells within me, that is, in my flesh" (Romans 7:18, PAR). But when the law or force of the spirit of life that is in Christ Jesus becomes a real presence in our body, that opens the way to liberation from the force of sin in our bodily parts (see Romans 7:23). The result is that the body increasingly becomes a major part of the hidden source from which our lives immediately flow.

You may wonder, *Won't the body naturally change its habits if the heart is transformed?* While a change of heart is primary, the outer change is not automatic. You work on inner and outer change concurrently, and each process informs the other. While we guard our heart and readjust it as needed, we also need to confront the body in its regimented habits. We teach our body to "fake it till we make it" (as the twelve-step saying goes) to help it behave according to what the heart is learning. To live a life of faking it is wrong, of course, and so we're always working through heart issues. While I'm learning to pray for the coworker who exasperates me (and therefore let my heart be changed), I ask God to help me regularly form my lips into a smile at that coworker. If I do this, I will be amazed at how that smile makes it easier for my heart to adjust.

◦❧ TODAY'S EXPERIMENT ❧◦

Pick one of your body movements that doesn't reflect the love, joy, and peace of Jesus. Don't start with something too big. Something like tapping your foot in impatience will do.

Choose what you could do instead. Perhaps you could try the humble stance of putting your hands behind your back. This makes it easier for the heart to be humble, which in turn makes it easier to stand that way.

At the same time, refocus your thoughts (and heart), perhaps praying Psalm 23 as we did earlier. Even as you theoretically "fake it," you can be authentically honest: "I'm operating on the theory that you, O Lord, really are my Shepherd, that you have provided everything I need, even though I have no idea what's going on." Picture that sheep lying in the green pasture so content, not needing a thing, even as you wait anxiously at a traffic signal thinking of your child waiting in the cold, as you lie on a gurney in an emergency room waiting for the nurse to return with the pain medication, or as you wait in line wondering why all these people chose to come to the same store at the same moment.

RELEASING THE BODY TO GOD

Certain steps can be taken so that the body can serve as a primary ally in Christlikeness. These steps help us "present our bodies as a living and holy sacrifice, very pleasing to God" (Romans 12:1, PAR). This total yielding of every part of our body to God, until the very tissues and muscles that make it up are inclined toward God and godliness, breaks all conformity with worldly life in this age. It transforms us into conformity with the age to come by completing the renewal of our mind—our powers of thought and imagination and judgment, which are deeply rooted in our body.

We must actually *release our body to God*. This needs to be a definite action, renewed as appropriate, perhaps on a yearly basis. But you will not drift into this position before God, and you will not stay there without decisive action. Take a day in silent and solitary retreat. Quiet your soul and your body and let them get clear of the fog of your daily burdens and preoccupations. Meditatively pray some central Scriptures before the Lord, especially those dealing directly with the body (see above; also Romans 8:5-14; 1 Corinthians 6:19-20; Colossians 3:5-10).

I recommend that you then lie on the floor, facedown or faceup, and formally surrender your body to God. Then go over the main parts of your body and do the same for each one. Ask God to *take charge* of your body and each part, to fill it with his life and use it for his purposes. Accentuate the positive; don't just think of not sinning with your body. You will find that increasing freedom will follow naturally from active consecration of your body to God's power and his purpose. Remember, a sacrifice is something *taken up* in God.

Give plenty of time to this ritual of sacrifice. Do not rush. When you are done, give God thanks. Arise and spend some time in praise. (An ecstatic reading—chant and walk or dance—of Psalms 145–150 would be an excellent exercise.) Put your *body* into it. Later, share what you have done with a spiritual friend or pastor and ask him or her to bless it. Review your ritual of sacrifice in thought and prayer from time to time over the following weeks and *plan* to renew the same ritual surrender year by year.

Perhaps the above sounds strange to you. You might wonder, *Can't I just think about doing it instead of going through this exercise?* If your desire is to retrain your body, you need to employ your body in the exercise. You may want to go back and rehearse your strongest and most frequent feelings in the mirror to see how your body responds to those feelings within you before doing this.

✧ TODAY'S EXPERIMENT ✧

As you lay your body down on the floor as on an altar before God, quiet yourself. Perhaps start with your eyes. Ask God to *take charge* of your eyes and to fill them with his life and use them for his purposes. Perhaps you want to ask God to keep your eyes from expressions of disgust or terror.

Then, ask God to show you what it would look like to offer love with your eyes: to impart compassion with your eyes, to reveal purpose with your eyes.

Do the same with other parts of your body such as your eyebrows and mouth, your shoulders, and your hands. What tilt of your head or position of your arms embodies love, compassion, or purpose?

In the future, as you read the Gospels, notice Jesus' bodily positions. What did he do with his hands? When and with whom did he squat? At what persons did he gaze? Use these questions to admire how Jesus offered love and purpose in his body.

40

MISUSES OF THE BODY

Here are some other things we can do to place our body and its parts fully at the disposal of the redeeming power of God living in us.

No longer idolize your body. Human ruin comes from placing ourselves at the center of our universe, in place of God. This leads to worship of the body and to a life of sensuality. Then our body becomes our primary source of gratification and the chief instrument for getting what we want. For most people, their body governs their life. Even professing Christians often devote to their spiritual growth only a tiny fraction of the time they devote to their body.

So no longer make the body an object of ultimate concern. You don't need to worry about what will happen to it—sickness, repulsiveness, aging, death—for you have placed God in charge of all that, and any issues that arise in this area you freely take up with him in prayer.

Do not misuse your body, especially as a source of sensual gratification or of domination or manipulation of others. Bodily pleasure is not in itself a bad thing, but when it is exalted to a necessity and we become dependent upon it, then we are slaves of our body and its feelings. Only misery lies ahead.

When we quit using our body to dominate or control others, we do not present our body in ways that elicit sexual thoughts, feelings, and actions from others. We do not try to be sexy. Giving up these things, of course, could be a fatal blow to the fashion industry and to other large segments of the economy, but we have to leave them to look after themselves.

Misusing the body also includes intimidation by means of our body. The most common forms of it are social, for example "power dressing," sarcasm, and "knowing" looks and remarks. Having given up our body to God, we do not then use it in these ways.

A group of people were recently asked to think of the most beautiful woman they knew. Without consulting each other, they didn't pick a glamorous celebrity. All of them picked women they knew who were much older and very wise. All the women chosen had gray hair! These people laughed to think that they associated beauty with gray hair, because aging and gray hair are so unpleasant to our culture but so honored in God's view (see Proverbs 16:31; 20:29).

ᙢ Today's Experiment ᙢ

Choose one of these three topics to journal about or at least ponder while you're driving:

- Consider how much time you spend on sprucing up your body—haircuts, grooming, buying body care products, shopping for clothes. What effect does spending this much time have on you? What messages are you sending to yourself (and your children)? How would you finish these sentences? I must look_____. I must dress_____.
- If you had just one change of clothes (which is what more than half of the people in the world have), how hard would that be for you? Think about how you look in the morning before you've arranged your hair. How hard would it be for you to live without a comb or other hair accessory?
- Consider why aging seems so negative in our culture and the supreme compliment it is to be told you look ten or twenty years younger than you are. Talk to God about how important (or unimportant) outward looks are to you. Ask God to show you how important it is to you that wisdom (sometimes) comes with age.
- What disciplines of simplicity or frugality in dress and appearance might be helpful to you?

41

SABBATH MOMENTS

The body must be properly cherished and cared for, not as our master, but as a servant of God. Our body is to be regarded as holy because it is owned and inhabited by God. So we give it proper nourishment, exercise, and rest.

Overwork misuses the body, but it has become the new "drug of choice." Often this is associated with excessive competition and trying to beat others in some area of life. Sometimes this is just a matter of wearing our body out in order to succeed. God *never* gives us too much to do. He long ago gave us these words: "It is vain for you to rise up early, to sit up late, to eat the bread of sorrows: for so he giveth his beloved sleep" (Psalm 127:2, KJV).

The practical center of proper care for the body is Sabbath. Sabbath is inseparable from worship, and, indeed, genuine worship is Sabbath. When we come to the place where we can joyously "do no work" (Leviticus 23:3, KJV), it will be because God has become so exalted in our mind and body that we can trust him with our lives and our world and can take our own hands off them.

For most of us, we can achieve Sabbath first in the practice of solitude and silence. We must carefully seek these disciplines by cultivating and dwelling in them. When they become established in our soul and our body, we can practice them in company with others. But the body *must* be weaned away from its tendencies to take control, to run the world, to achieve and produce, to attain gratification.

Rest is one primary mark of the condition of Sabbath in the body, as unrest is a primary mark of its absence. So if we really intend to submit our body as a living sacrifice to God, our first step might well be to start *getting enough sleep.* Sleep is a good first use of solitude and silence. It is also a good indicator of how thoroughly we trust in God.

A pastor friend of mine explained that he had to take a two-week vacation because it took him an entire week to wind down. Then he could enjoy the second week. How long does it take for your body to wind all the way down like a windup clock that stops only after the daily winding of it ceases? When a body is practiced in Sabbath keeping, it can enter into unhurried peace at the drop of a hat—drifting off to sleep in a waiting room, soaking in the sun's rays on a bench at a soccer field, enjoying stillness even when waiting at a traffic signal.

But in the beginning of developing such a habit, the body rebels. So we cultivate customary ways to "Sabbath" ourselves down—discovering the settings, the props, and the important preliminary steps that help (for example, not overscheduling ourselves). Don't be concerned that your steps are small; just be determined to take them.

❧ TODAY'S EXPERIMENT ☙

Consider what your next step is in advancing a Sabbath practice for your body. What kind of solitude and silence are you ready to attempt: a morning without your cell phone, an afternoon in the park, a fast from all media for a week, a one-day retreat, an extended retreat? At first, each of these may feel as if you're giving up something precious, but it won't take long to see that you have gained much more than you have given up. You will have given your body space to unlearn its tricks of hurry, competition, achievement, and manipulation. It will have tasted that sense of abiding with God.

42

FORMATION IS NOT PRIVATE

Spiritual formation, good or bad, is always profoundly social. You cannot keep it to yourself. Anyone who says, "It's just between me and God" has misunderstood God as well as "me." Relationships must be transformed if we are to be transformed. Jesus gave a sure mark of the outcome of spiritual formation: We become people who love one another (see John 13:35). This love is not unspecified: "*Just as I have loved you*, you also should love one another" (verse 34, NRSV, emphasis added). The "love" in question here is identified as *what we do in Christ, as he has done for us*. This love makes us ready to "lay down our lives for the brethren" (1 John 3:16).

Failure to love others as Jesus loves us chokes off the flow of the eternal kind of life that our whole human system cries out for (see 1 John 3:14). To welcome others, to make a place for them and provide for them, is one of the most life-giving and life-receiving things a human being can do. These are the basic, universal acts of love. Our lives were meant to be full of such acts, drawing on the abundance of God.

Such love is possible because of what God is: love. The profoundly good news is not just that *God loves us*. A pretty mean person can love someone for special reasons (see Matthew 5:46-47). But God *is* love and sustains love *for us* from his basic reality as love, which dictates his Trinitarian nature. God is in himself a sweet society of love where three persons complete a social matrix. Not only does each one love and receive love, but each has a *shared* love for another, the third person. The nature of personality is inherently communal, and only the Trinity does justice to what personality is.

This sort of love is meant to happen *routinely* among God's people.

In the church as the body of Christ, members nourish one another with the transcendent power that raised up Christ from the dead and now flows through each member to the others.

Try to picture a church board meeting, committee meeting, or parking lot discussion governed by this self-giving, self-perpetuating love. You and I would love each other with Christlike love, and together we would love the third person with us. Wouldn't everyone *want* to be a Christian? Wouldn't wounded people flock to our church?

Such love, however, involves an openhanded death: "This is how we know what love is: Jesus Christ laid down his life for us. And we ought to *lay down our lives* for our brothers" (1 John 3:16, NIV, emphasis added). We will have to die to ourselves—to the desire to be first, to control, to be admired, to be sought after. For "we are dead and our life is hid with Christ in God. When Christ, who is our life, shall be revealed, then we will be revealed with him, glorious" (Colossians 3:3-4, PAR). But what could be better than being "hid with Christ in God?" That's exactly where a person in union with God would want to be. As we die to ourselves, we come to participate in a resurrected sort of life (see Philippians 3:11). With such a Jesus-based way of life, we become one who nourishes and cherishes the person next to us.

✎ TODAY'S EXPERIMENT ✎

Consider how you need to lay yourself down as on an altar in order to nourish others. How do you need to interact with others in order to lay down your life for them? Look back through this book at sentences you have marked. What does laying down your life involve? Perhaps desires, thoughts, and habits, such as interrupting or insisting on your own way? What disciplines is God calling you to?

Pray, thanking God for this possibility of living a resurrected sort of life that will extend life-giving love to others, especially in church situations. Ask God to keep showing you not only what you need to lay down but also how to live that resurrected sort of life in Christ.

CHAPTER

43

RECIPROCAL ROOTEDNESS
IN OTHERS

Those spiritually formed in Christlikeness find the natural condition of life to be one of reciprocal rootedness in others. Stable, healthy living requires the assurance of others being *for* us. We are told in the earliest pages of the Bible that "it is not good that the man should be alone," so God decided to make "a helper to be a match for him" (Genesis 2:18, PAR). Centuries later Paul pointed out that "not one of us lives unto himself and not one dies unto himself" (Romans 14:7, PAR). Human beings are really *together* only in God, and all other ways of "being with" fall short of the needs of basic human nature.

If this assurance of others being *for* us is not there, we are but walking wounded. Our lives will more or less be in shambles until we die. Dealing with the spiritual formation of our social dimension begins with this *woundedness*. A child who is not adequately received in this world is likely to be incapable of giving and receiving love in decent human relationships for the rest of his life. He will be perpetually left out, if only in his imagination. And in this matter, imagination can have the force of reality.

Severe wounds to our rootedness may also occur in later life. Various failures can bring rejection or detachment from parents and other significant figures. Unfaithfulness in a mate, divorce, failure in career advancement, disloyalty of children, or just never making it "in"[4] may leave us disconnected from others. Lack of nourishment from deep connections with others means spiritual starvation in our every dimension.

But if a child is totally received in his early years by his parents and siblings, he will likely have a rootedness about him that will enable him to withstand most forms of rejection that may come upon a human being. He will carry his solid relationships to and from his family members throughout life, being sustained by them even long after those loved ones are dead. He will receive a steady stream of rest and strength from them.

If you've been wounded by others, you may find the idea of "reciprocal rootedness in others" scary. Being wounded may have taught you to be self-contained, to get your needs met anyway *you* can because no one else will help you. Without a full realization of God's enfolding love and power, no combination of information or guidance or affection can prevent or heal wounds. Without God, we can at best become hardened and simply carry on.

The primary *other* for a human being, whether we understand it or not, is always God. So even though we risk and venture out into relationships (as part of the spiritual formation of our soul), we don't put all our eggs in another person's basket; we put them in God's basket. We commit ourselves to God, and with God's leading we reach out to another. We don't expect this other person to necessarily nurture us. We go to God for nurture. Now and then, God may use that other person to nurture us, but we receive it as from God. *The Lord really is our Shepherd*—even in relationships.

⁓ TODAY'S EXPERIMENT ⁓

Consider risking a little and inviting to lunch (or some similar setting) someone who might be relatively new to you or with whom you have not interacted for a long time. Instead of thinking about what you might receive or what may happen, pray beforehand that God will work within the situation to bless both of you. If things turn out differently from what you would have liked (he says no to your invitation, she invites a third party, and so on), trust that God will work through this.

Pray for that person before you meet, asking God to show you what you need to know to bless this person. As you converse, enjoy yourself but silently call God's blessing on that person now and then. Afterward, ask God again to bless both you and that person, acknowledging that none of us lives unto our own self, nor do we die unto our own self.

How Lovelessness Works

Sin in our social dimension takes two forms of lovelessness: *assault* (attack) and *withdrawal* (distancing). If spiritual formation in Christ is to succeed, the power of assault and withdrawal *must* be broken so they are eliminated as *indwelling realities* or as *postures* we take toward others. They also must be successfully disarmed as they come toward us. They must be eliminated in our social environment—family or household, those with whom we work or play, our community—but especially in the fellowships of Christ's followers.

We *assault* others when we *act against what is good for them*, even with their consent. The more well-known forms of assault are dealt with in the last six of the Ten Commandments—murder, adultery, theft, and so on. We *withdraw* from others when we are indifferent to their well-being or perhaps even despise them. We "don't care." Withdrawal is usually a form of assaulting those we withdraw from. And assault usually involves distancing ourselves as well.

Spiritual formation in Christ will mean becoming persons who *would not* (and therefore do not) assault others. A verbal assault (which can be done in refined as well as brutal ways—we speak of a "cutting remark") is specifically designed to hurt its object and to inflict loss of respect in a person's own eyes and before others. Many people never recover from a particular verbal assault, harassment, or degrading treatment. Most often this happens to people while very young or otherwise weak and unprotected. But withdrawal also wounds. The tongue can assault by withdrawal, by not speaking.

As assault and withdrawal are eliminated, the social area of our lives becomes what God intended: a play of constant mutual blessing.

Every contact with a human being should be one of goodwill and respect, with a *readiness* to make way for the other in suitable ways.

Perhaps you know someone who has a habit of being sarcastic or making a cutting remark or pointing out whatever is wrong about your clothing today. I have been that person. Several years ago, I started this experiment: What if I were to pray for a person each time I criticized that person to someone else or even only in my mind?

This had several effects. First, it slowed me down so much that criticism became a rather time-consuming chore. In that slower mode, I saw that perhaps my criticism was inaccurate. In praying for the person, I experienced such repentance for what I said that I became miserable. I didn't enjoy being with myself. So why not use the time spent in criticism praying for that person to begin with or even shifting my thoughts entirely — say, to thanking God for that wildflower popping up out of the crack in the sidewalk?

⤳ TODAY'S EXPERIMENT ⤶

Pretend you've been hired as a "detective angel" to watch yourself and analyze your usual methods of attack and withdrawal. Your imaginary boss wants to know about X (you): Does X usually attack or withdraw? Toward which people or sorts of people? What feelings within X are most likely to create the urge to attack or withdraw? When does X withdraw so X wants to *appear* too nice to attack? What are X's preferred phrases of attack/withdrawal? Finally, what is at the root of X's perceived need to attack or withdraw (fear, resentment, contempt, jealousy)? Make a preliminary report as best you can, promising to deliver more as the days go by.

As you listen to your report, picture yourself in Psalm 23:5. You sit at a table uniquely prepared for you. Sitting across from you is an enemy or two (people who make life difficult), poised for attack (or withdrawal as their form of attack). Now picture God anointing your head with oil — signifying your special usefulness to him. Notice how your cup is always full so that you feel secure and you never look inadequate to that enemy. If you can do it, try to grin in blessing at your enemy instead of attacking.

45

LETTING GO OF
ATTACK AND WITHDRAWAL

Especially in our families and friendships, we must identify how assault and withdrawal defeat love. We can break away from these tendencies by learning a calm but firm noncooperation with those poisonous elements and by making initiatives of goodwill and blessing in the midst of such attacks. What we do when we meet as Christians should equip us to do this effectively elsewhere.

Attack and withdrawal can render persons (even professing Christians) incapable of a positive marriage — giving oneself to another person, supporting this person for good in his or her life in every way possible (see Ephesians 5:22-33). It is not these persons' fault. In this world, how could they know how to do this? In modern life, *individual desire has come to be the standard and rule of everything.* How are we to *serve* one another if desire is the standard and if what we desire can be acquired from many others besides our spouse?

The spiritual malformation of children is an inevitable result. Their souls, bodies, and minds absorb the assault and withdrawal of their parents, who are constantly engaged with their children. They are soon attacked and frozen out, too. Their only hope of survival is to maintain a constant posture of withdrawal. These hardened, lonely souls, readied for addiction, aggression, isolation, and self-destructive behavior, turn to their bodies for self-gratification and to control others, or for isolation and self-destruction.

Such children grow up to be malfunctioning souls in their workplace, professions, citizenship, and leadership. Many of them try to rectify the situation by working for solutions to the human problem, such as education or diversity or tolerance. These things are good, but they do not come close to the root of the human problem. Ignorance, prejudice, or intolerance draw upon the still deeper-lying soul structures of assault and withdrawal, which feed those negative influences.

So to heal the open sore of social existence, congregations of apprentices to Jesus must return to the transcendent power of Christ in which they stand. They must *drain the assault and withdrawal, the attack and coldness, from the individual men and women who form families under their ministry of Jesus and his kingdom.*

Perhaps families are the most frequent scene of attack because there the true self emerges. And perhaps we don't check ourselves because we know we can get away with it there. Instead of giving our best to those we deeply love, we may give them our worst.

Our hope for change comes through participating in a life from above, which connects us to that invisible spiritual realm and its powers (see John 3:8). We really do have "everything we need for life and godliness." How? "Through our knowledge of him who called us by his own glory and goodness" (2 Peter 1:3, NIV). Experiment with such knowledge of him.

◈ TODAY'S EXPERIMENT ◈

Picture Jesus teaching in the synagogue on the Sabbath. Imagine a bent-over woman who had been crippled for eighteen years. As so often happened, his overwhelming compassion beamed toward her. He called her up front and said, "Woman, you are set free from your infirmity" (Luke 13:12, NIV). Can you see Jesus gently putting his hands on this dear woman so that in an instant she stretched herself out tall and statuesque, shouting out praise to God?

Into this moment of joy and wonder entered an indignant synagogue leader to say that Jesus picked the wrong day to heal her. This was not a Lord's Day sort of thing to do.

Set aside what really happened next and instead imagine Jesus attacking this leader in the clever way we know he could have — lightning bolts coming out of the clouds, melting the man (recall the wicked witch at the end of *The Wizard of Oz*), or simply ignoring him but later using his influence to make sure he never ate lunch in that town again.

In reality, Jesus did speak up, indicting such behavior as hypocrisy and asserting that this dear woman was more important than the man's livestock, which he would have gladly rescued had it been imperiled on the Sabbath (see Luke 13:10-16).

See how Jesus embodied this calm but firm noncooperation with those who attacked him? He did not take things personally but addressed the specific issue. I imagine that if he saw the synagogue leader in the marketplace the next day, he may have bought him a kumquat and drawn him in affable conversation. What do you think Jesus would have done?

46

STEPS TOWARD GENUINE LOVE

The first element in the spiritual formation of our social dimension is for individuals to come to *see themselves whole*, as God himself sees them—to regard themselves as blessed no matter what has happened. This vision of wholeness in God draws the poisons from our relationships with others and enables us to go forward with sincere forgiveness and blessing toward them. Only in this way can we stand free from the wounds of the past and from those who have assaulted or forsaken us.

The second element is *abandonment of all defensiveness*. This includes a willingness to be known in our most intimate relationships for who we really are. It includes abandonment of practices of self-justification, evasiveness, and deceit, as well as manipulation. We do not hide, and we do not follow strategies for "looking good."

As pretense vanishes from our lives, the third element in this transformation of the self comes forward: *love among Christians that is "genuine"* (Romans 12:9, NRSV). Love characterizes local gatherings of disciples (churches) so that each person carries out her particular work in the group life with a grace and power that is not from herself but from God (see Romans 12:3-8).

The fourth element is to *extend ourselves in blessing and redemption* to all whose lives we touch. Without the burden of defending ourselves, we can act from the resources of our new life from above and devote our lives to the service of others.

Such formation in Christ requires that we increasingly be happily reconciled to living by the direct upholding of the hand of God. Certainly, to achieve this in our social dimension we must have heard and accepted the gospel of grace: of Jesus' defenseless death on the cross on our behalf and of his acceptance of us into his life beyond the worst that could be done to him or to us. We must stand safe and solid in his kingdom.

After describing how the body of Christ works together in grace and power (see Romans 12:3-8), Paul described Christ's body behaving this way (verses 9-21):

- Letting love be completely real.
- Abhorring what is evil.
- Clinging to what is good.
- Being devoted to one another in family-like love.
- Outdoing one another in giving honor.
- Serving the Lord with an ardent spirit and in all diligence.
- Rejoicing in hope.
- Being patient in troubles.
- Being devoted constantly to prayer.
- Contributing to the needs of the saints.
- Pursuing (running after) hospitality.
- Blessing persecutors and not cursing them.
- Being joyful with those who are rejoicing and being sorrowful with those in sorrow.
- Living in harmony with each other.
- Not being haughty, but fitting right in with the lowly, in human terms.
- Not seeing oneself as wise.
- Never repaying evil for evil.
- Having due regard for what everyone takes to be right.
- Being at peace with everyone, so far as it depends on you.
- Never taking revenge, but leaving that to whatever God may decide.
- Providing for needy enemies.
- Not being overwhelmed by evil, but overwhelming evil with good.

◈ TODAY'S EXPERIMENT ◈

Imagine yourself as part of a group of disciples of Jesus who made this list their shared intention and actually lived it out. Your group would operate as a small group or even as a church and do the normal things that groups do, but effort and discussion would be focused on doing those things as described above. Perhaps every group meeting would begin by savoring God's grace and power and envisioning life together such as this. All planning would flow from these goals.

What would marriages in such a group be like? How would that congregation interact with its community? How would disagreements be solved?

What would you like most about such a group? What aspect of love (listed above) would you cherish most in that group? How would you be changed by experiencing a group such as this? Seeing yourself as whole? Abandoning defensiveness? Extending yourself in blessing to others?

To what group is God calling you to be such a group member today?

47

INTEGRATING THE
DIMENSIONS OF THE SELF

At any moment it is your soul that is running your life. Not thoughts, intentions, or feelings, but your soul. The soul is that aspect that *integrates* the dimensions of the self and how they interact with each other. The soul lies almost totally beyond conscious awareness.

In the person with a well-kept heart, the soul is properly ordered under God and in harmony with reality. The outcome is a person who is *capable* of responding to the situations of life in ways that are good and right, such as the person in Psalm 1. He does not determine his course of action by what those without God say—even their latest brilliant ideas. Living within only human "wisdom" makes it "necessary" to do what is wrong and to prepare explanations of why one who does wrong things is still a good person and why those who do otherwise are fools. This person is an expert scorner, putting others in their place with appropriate doses of contempt, which is an essential element of scorn (see verse 1).

In contrast, the Psalm 1 person *delights* in the law that God has given. He dwells upon it, turning it over and over in his mind and speaking it to himself. It is where his whole being is oriented.

For many, this ideal arrangement of life under God remains an impossible dream, for their soul is running amuck and their life is in chaos. Enslaved to their desires or their bodily habits, or blinded by false ideas, their soul cannot find its way into a life of consistent truth and harmonious pursuit of what is good.

The individual soul's formation is seen in how thoughts, feelings, social relations, bodily behaviors, and choices unfold, and especially how they interact with each other. Many times an individual is in deep self-conflict. However, one must not underestimate the powers of recovery of the soul under grace. God is over all. The soul manifests amazing capacities for recovery when it finds its home in God and receives his grace.

Perhaps you know what it's like to have thoughts, feelings, social relations, bodily behaviors, and choices that conflict with each other. You know what you should do, but you don't *feel* like doing it. You want to say gracious, kind things, but your tongue takes over with sarcasm. Before you leave home, you decide to treat a certain relative with grace, but once you get to the family gathering and that person makes a catty remark about you, you stay exiled in another room for the rest of the day.

What would it take to be like a fruit-bearing, unwitherable tree planted by streams of water? What is needed for you to prosper naturally?

❧ TODAY'S EXPERIMENT ❧

Ponder the scriptural images in these two passages:

> "Cursed is the one who trusts in man,
>   who depends on flesh [natural capabilities] for his strength
>   and whose heart turns away from the LORD.
> He will be like a bush in the wastelands;
>   he will not see prosperity when it comes.
> He will dwell in the parched places of the desert,
>   in a salt land where no one lives." (Jeremiah 17:5-6, NIV)

Why does depending on natural capabilities turn one's heart from God? Why would such a person not see prosperity when it's standing right in front of him?

What are the parched places in your life? How are you like this bush?

> "But blessed is the man who trusts in the LORD,
> whose confidence is in him.
> He will be like a tree planted by the water
> that sends out its roots by the stream.
> It does not fear when heat comes;
> its leaves are always green.
> It has no worries in a year of drought
> and never fails to bear fruit." (verses 7-8, NIV)

What does this person not fear? How would you have to arrange your life differently in order to be a person whose roots thrust out toward the stream that is God?

What do these verses lead you to pray?

48

THE DEPTHS OF OUR BEING

Our soul is like an inner stream of water, which gives strength, direction, and harmony to every other element of our lives. When that stream is as it should be, we are constantly refreshed and exuberant in all we do, because our soul itself is then profusely rooted in the vastness of God and his kingdom, including nature. All else within us is enlivened and directed by that stream. Therefore, we are in harmony with God, reality, and the rest of human nature and nature at large.

To refer to someone's soul is to say something about the ultimate depths of his being. Consider Jesus' teaching that it does not profit one to gain the whole world and lose his own soul (see Matthew 16:26). What does it mean to lose your soul? Can you actually do that? Does it describe anyone you know? What it means is that your whole life is no longer under the direction of your inner stream of life, which has been taken over by exteriors. For example, the rich farmer abandoned his soul in favor of externalities. He had laid up treasure for himself and was not "rich toward God" (Luke 12:21). On the positive side, we see Mary calling upon her soul, that is, the deepest part of her being, to "magnify the Lord" (Luke 1:46, KJV).

The psalmist said,

My soul thirsts for You, my flesh yearns for You,
In a dry and weary land where there is no water. (Psalm 63:1)

Of course the "water" spoken of here is not H_2O but the water of life, which Jesus promised. These and many other passages make clear that the soul is the most basic level of life in the individual and is by nature rooted in God. We must take care to do whatever we can to keep it in his hands, recognizing all the while that we can do this only with his help.

John Wesley was famous for asking the question, "How is it with your soul?" Such a question requires reflection because the soul resides in the depths of our being. That reflection requires not so much concentration but a quieting of self so that the soul's condition can be discerned.

When speaking of our soul, we can borrow ideas and language from the Psalms, which show us how to talk about and to our soul. Look at the various states of the psalmists' soul: the soul is *in anguish* (see 6:3), is *consumed with longing* for God's laws (see 119:20), and is *weary with sorrow* (see 119:28). Notice the things the soul does: *pants* for God (see 42:1), *thirsts* for God (see 42:2; 63:1), *finds rest* in God (see 62:1), *clings* to God (see 63:8), *longs and yearns* for the courts of God (see 84:2), and *waits* for God (see 130:5). The psalmist even *talks* to his or her soul, asking questions:

> Why are you downcast, O my soul?
>> Why so disturbed within me? (42:5, NIV)

Then the psalmist tells the soul what to do:

> Put your hope in God,
>> for I will yet praise him,
>> my Savior and my God. (42:5, NIV)

> Awake, my soul! (57:8, NIV)

> Find rest, O my soul, in God alone. (62:5, NIV)

> Praise the LORD, O my soul;
>> all my inmost being. (103:1, NIV)

Perhaps most touching, the psalmist *asks God* to say to his or her soul: "I am your salvation" (35:3, NIV).

⚘ Today's Experiment ⚘

Ponder how it is with your soul, using questions such as these:

- What state is your soul in (anguish, longing for God's justice, at rest)?
- What does your soul repeatedly do (pant, thirst for God, wait for God, rail against God)?
- What question would you like to ask your soul? (Why are you downcast? Why are you distracted?)
- What would you like to say to your soul? (Hope in God. Find rest.)
- What would you like God to say to your soul? (I am your hope. I hear you. I come alongside you.)

THE CRIES OF THE SOUL

In spiritual transformation, it is necessary to take the soul seriously and deal with it regularly and intelligently, to be mindful of it. Yet you hear little about the soul in Christian groups, and you see few people seriously concerned about the state of their own soul.

Some people talk about *saving* the soul, but once the soul is "safe," it is usually treated as needing no further attention. Ignoring the soul is one reason Christian churches have become fertile sources of recruits for cults and other religious and political groups. We may dimly discern our own soul's condition and that of others, but we rarely can articulate those conditions and comprehend them at a level required for reflection and discussion. This is not compatible with the serious undertaking of spiritual formation. We as individuals must "own" our souls and take responsibility before God for them, turning to our pastors and teachers for the necessary help.

Once we clearly acknowledge the soul, we can learn to *hear its cries*. Jesus heard its cries from the wearied humanity he saw around him. The multitudes around him tore his heart, for they were "distressed and dispirited like sheep without a shepherd" (Matthew 9:36). He invited such people to come and become his students ("learn of me," Matthew 11:29, KJV) by yoking themselves to him—that is, letting him show them how he would pull their load. He is not above this, as earthly "great ones" are, for he is "meek and lowly in heart" (Matthew 11:29, KJV).

His own greatness of soul made meekness and lowliness the natural way for him to be (see Philippians 2:3-11). Being in his yoke is not a matter of taking on additional labor to crush us all the more, but a matter of learning how to use his strength *and* ours together to bear our load *and* his. We will find his yoke an easy one and his burden a light one *because*, in learning from him, we have found rest for our soul. Rest *for* our soul is rest *in* God. Our soul is at peace only when it is with God, as a child with its mother.

Perhaps all this talk about the soul is getting too ethereal for you. Talking to one's soul? Really? But don't give up. The Psalms offer another (perhaps simpler) doorway through which we can encounter our soul.

❧ TODAY'S EXPERIMENT ☙

Choose an image from the Psalms below that best describes your soul and the things it wants to cry out. If you can't decide, choose the one your best friend or spouse would choose for you.

- A panting deer who has been running in search of water for a long time (see 42:1)
- A small creature crouching in the protective shadow of a huge creature (God's wings) (see 57:1)
- A weary desert traveler (see 63:1)
- A desert valley with huge dry cracks opening up (see 143:6)
- An ailing patient who stretches out his hands for help yet refuses to be comforted when comfort is offered (see 77:2)
- Someone who has narrowly escaped death (see 116:8)
- A tired mountain climber who has found a solid foothold (see 94:18-19)
- A guard on duty all night long (see 130:6)
- A wild and crazy musician who even talks to her instruments (see 108:1)
- A gourmet diner (see 63:5)
- A weaned child at his mother's breast—content and not even looking for food (see 131:2)

Consider the image you've chosen. What is the cry of your soul based on that image? What is needed to help your soul rest in God?

Think also of someone close to you, perhaps someone you minister to and hope to be a blessing to. Which image fits that person? What is the cry of his or her heart? How might you reach out to that person?

CHAPTER

50

ABANDONING OUTCOMES

As we take on Jesus' yoke, we abandon *outcomes* to God, accepting that we do not have the wherewithal to make life come out right. Even if we "suffer according to the will of God," we "entrust [our] souls to a faithful Creator in doing what is right" (1 Peter 4:19). This is the lowliness of heart learned in his yoke. What rest comes with it!

Humility is the framework within which all virtue lives. "Therefore humble yourselves under the mighty hand of God, that He may exalt you at the proper time, casting all your anxiety on Him, because He cares for you" (1 Peter 5:6-7). Humility, which involves losing our self-sufficiency, is a secret of soul rest because it does not presume to secure outcomes.

On the other hand, *pride* is the root of disobedience. We think we are "big enough" to take our lives into our own hands, and so we disobey what we know to be right. This *distances* us from God and forces us to live on our own. Soul rest becomes impossible.

Thus, fleshly lust wages war against the soul (see 1 Peter 2:11) by enticing us to uproot our dependent life, pulling it away from God, which will deprive our soul of what it needs to enliven and regulate our whole being. To allow lust (or strong desires) to govern our lives is to exalt our will over God's.

That is why Paul called covetousness *idolatry* (see Ephesians 5:5; Colossians 3:5). We have become the idol, and we are prepared to sacrifice the well-being and possessions of others to our self-interest. Arrogant wrongdoing is the deepest possible wound one can inflict on another's soul.

When living in the cradle of humility, we understand that God has a plan for our lives that goes far beyond anything *we* can work out. We simply rest in his life as he gives it to us. While resting in God, we can be free from all anxiety, which means deep soul rest. We don't fret or get angry because others seem to be doing better than we are, even though we think they might be less deserving than we are.

Our teenage daughter left home and for three years lived either on the streets or with various people who took her in. Although we received wise counsel from a support group for parents of troubled teens, we had other friends who patted me on the hand and said, "Don't worry. She'll come home." I didn't think this was wise comfort. Because I have volunteered with the homeless, I know that not everyone comes home. Who was to say what my daughter would choose?

That advice would have encouraged me to trust in outcomes, to trust that *my faith* would somehow *force certain results* from my daughter and from God. I couldn't do that. Although I felt very confident in God, I didn't feel confident about my friends' prescribed outcomes. I didn't trust that our daughter would get a job or change her living situation. I trusted God. I asked God for those things, but I didn't trust in those results. God could be my comfort and strength without my telling God what to do. (She did come home and made an impressive turnaround.)

✎ TODAY'S EXPERIMENT ✎

What expectations are you holding on to? Can you still trust God even if X never happens? If a certain job or living situation or relationship doesn't work out, are you still able to delight in this God who loves you tremendously?

If your desires (or, more specifically, *you*) are the idol of your soul, consider how you could begin to give that up. Try saying this prayer and see if you're on the journey of it being authentic: "I trust you, O God. I want to simply rest in *your* life as *you* give it to me. Show me how to be at peace, even when others who are less deserving seem to do better than I do. Help me look to the heavens and exclaim, 'Surely goodness and mercy *will follow* me all the days of my life. I'm thrilled to dwell in your house, O God, forever.'"

THE SWEETNESS OF THE LAW

Efforts at spiritual formation in Christlikeness must reverse the process of distancing the soul from God and bring it back into union with him. *The law of God can help us do that.*

The written law God gave the Israelites is one of the greatest gifts of grace God has conveyed to the human race. It was given as a meeting place between God and human beings in covenant relationship with him, where the sincere heart would be received, instructed, and enabled by God to walk in his ways. When those walking in personal relationship with him receive, study, and internalize his law into their heart, it quickens and restores connection and order to the flagging soul.

Viewing the law as something we can or must achieve (self-idolatry), however, repeats the degradation of the law committed by the Pharisees at the time of Jesus. It is turned from a pathway of grace to an instrument of cultural self-righteousness and human oppression.

Today, we in the Western world live in an *antinomian* culture. (*Antinomian* means "against the law.") This tendency is based upon the mistaken conclusion—rejected by Paul—that since we are not *justified* by keeping the law but rather through our personal relationship of confidence in Jesus, we have no essential use for the law and can disregard it. This tendency annuls the law, which is what Jesus said not to do (see Matthew 5:19). The presence of the Spirit and of grace is not meant to set the law aside but to *enable conformity to it from an inwardly transformed personality.*

The "royal law" of love (James 2:8), abundantly spelled out in Jesus and his teaching, includes all that was essential in the older law, which he fulfilled and enables us to fulfill through constant discipleship to him. One whose aim is anything less than obedience to the law of God in the Spirit and power of Jesus will never have a soul at rest in God and will never advance significantly in spiritual transformation into Christlikeness.

Perhaps you see how your soul is not in union with God, and you would like to reverse the process of distancing your soul from God. But is it realistic to *delight* in the law (see Psalm 1:2)?

One way the law becomes sweet to us is in our repentance after disregarding it. We have all behaved in loveless ways—attacking someone or distancing ourselves, getting involved in an unhealthy attraction, shooting off our mouth when we should have been quiet (see Matthew 5:39-47,27-28,33-37). In our grief we see how we acted in self-interest and used or disregarded the other person. We were not patient and kind; we were proud, easily irritated, and did not protect the other person (see 1 Corinthians 13:4-5,7). As we "think about our thinking" (one way of translating repentance, *metanoia*), we see that God's law really is good and wise. Goodness and wisdom embrace the difficult person, they treat an attractive person with respect (instead of lust), and they speak simply.

It is a deep blessing to meet someone who does these things. Then you see God's goodness in the simplicity of genuine love. You want that transformation in yourself. To be that way would bring the sparkle of gold and the sweetness of honey to your soul.

❧ TODAY'S EXPERIMENT ☙

Give *delighting* in the law a try, perhaps by praying phrases from Psalm 1:1-2 or Psalm 119:7-11. The following are examples of how this might sound.

> *Blest am I when I stop listening to the voices of wickedness or posturing myself as a know-it-all. I find I can really love people*

when I delight in God's law, when I am thrilled by it, when I can't keep my mind off it. It is a beautiful, strong, and wise picture of reality—of what God, the spouse of my soul, is like.

This all-encompassing law can revive my languishing soul! The ideas in the law are ones I can trust, and they will help me "wise up" from my foolish ways! Their rightness is deep and will bring that longed-for joy to my heart. The radiant law will take the blinders off my eyes so that my habitual ways of responding will change. By absorbing these ideas I will have a purity of heart I have seen in so few people. Finally—I will have sureness in my steps. Oh, how I cling to these ideas! How I relish them! What a blessing they are to me from God!

Respond to God in whatever way seems appropriate—perhaps praying, journaling, singing, or dancing.

52

CHILDREN OF LIGHT

According to the biblical picture, the function of human history is to bring forth an immense community of people, from "every nation and tribe and tongue and people" (Revelation 14:6), who will be a kingdom of priests under God. They will reign with him in the eternal future of the cosmos forever and ever (see 1:6; 4:9; 5:10; 14:6; 22:5).

These people will, together as a living community, form a special dwelling place for God. What the human heart now vaguely senses *should* be eventually *will* be in the cosmic triumph of Christ and his people. Those "children of light" will be empowered by God in eternity to do what they want, as free creative agents. Spiritual formation in Christlikeness during our lives here on earth is a constant movement toward this eternal appointment.

Here and now the children of light are remarkably different, not in the things they do or don't do, though their behavior, too, is very different and distinctive. Children of light differ on the "inside" of their life.

Thought life: They love to dwell upon God's greatness and loveliness as brought to light in Jesus Christ. They adore God in nature, in history, in his Son, and in his saints. One could even say they are "God-intoxicated" (see Acts 2:13; Ephesians 5:18). They do not dwell upon evil. It is not a big thing in their thoughts. They are sure of its defeat. Because their mind is centered upon God, all other good things are also welcome there: "whatever is true, whatever is honorable, whatever is right, whatever is pure, whatever is lovely, whatever is of good repute" (Philippians 4:8).

Feelings: They love other people. They love their own life and who they are. They are thankful for their life even though it may contain many difficulties. They receive all of it as God's gift, or at least as his allowance. And so joy and peace are with them even in the hardest of times, even when suffering unjustly. Because of what they have learned about God, they are confident and hopeful and do not indulge thoughts of rejection, failure, and hopelessness, *because they know better*.

People sometimes complain that they aren't sure they would want to go to heaven. Who wants to play a harp? Even religious folks will admit they're not sure they want to sing all the time.

So they are surprised to hear the above ideas from Revelation, especially that we will have work that grips and absorbs us completely (to "reign" with God). We will *love* being the dwelling place of God and belonging to the living community we have always longed for. We will experience enormous beauty.

This helps us understand why spiritual formation here on earth is so important. We are being readied for a life we could never have believed possible.

✎ TODAY'S EXPERIMENT ✎

Talk to God regarding your thoughts about heaven, especially these ideas:

- Having union with him and being his dwelling place (see John 14:23; 15:4-5)
- Having a job or responsibility that uses everything within you, yet delights you
- Being empowered by him to do what you want, as a "free creative agent"

Does it seem odd for God to *believe in you* this way? Tell him that and ask him to help you see yourself with the eyes of faith.

Reflect on how these ideas affect your attitude toward spiritual formation into Christlikeness. How does "God-intoxication" create conditions of love, joy, peace, confidence, and hope?

53

WHAT CHILDREN OF LIGHT ARE LIKE

Walk as children of light (for the fruit of light consists in all goodness and righteousness and truth), verifying what is pleasing to the Lord" (Ephesians 5:8-10, PAR). Children of light differ from others on the "inside of their life" in these following ways also.

Will (also called spirit or heart): Children of light do not hesitate to do what they know to be good and right. They do not think first of themselves and what they want, and they really care very little about getting their own way. "Let each of you regard one another as more important than himself; do not look out for your own personal interests, but for the interests of others" (Philippians 2:3-4, PAR). They are abandoned to God's will and do not deliberate as to whether they will do what they know to be wrong.

Body: Their body is constantly *poised* to do what is right and good without thinking. They are not always trapped by what their tongue, facial expressions, and hands have *already* done before they can think. They avoid paths of temptation. Their body is even different. They have a freshness about them, a kind of quiet strength, and a transparency. They are rested and playful in a bodily strength that is from God.

Social relations: They are completely transparent. Because they walk in goodness, they achieve real contact with others, especially other apprentices of Jesus. They do not conceal their thoughts and feelings or try to manipulate and manage others. While they will not participate in evil, they are noncondemning.

Soul: All of the above is not just at the surface. It is deep and effortless. It *flows.*

When those who have become children of light are found to be wrong, they will never defend it. They are thankful to be found out (see Proverbs 9:8). Indeed, when accused of being in the wrong when they are not, they will not defend *themselves* but will say only as much as is required to prevent misunderstanding of the good. The meaning of being *justified* by grace alone has penetrated to every pore of their being.

This is the outcome of spiritual formation in Christlikeness.

Children of light are easy to deal with. We don't have to guess what game they're playing or what role they're assuming. They don't try to manipulate others. Even better, they don't judge. It isn't necessary to say to children of light, "I didn't want to give you the impression that . . ." or "I didn't want you to think . . ." because they've given up preoccupation with forming opinions about others. I don't need to brood, thinking, *I wonder what they thought of me!* Their transparency keeps me from wondering what their hidden agenda might have been because they simply don't have one. With children of light, everything is given to the care of God.

To some, this may sound boring. But remember that "they are rested and playful in a bodily strength that is from God." Often these people are more fun because there is no agenda behind their humor.

The road to becoming such a person—a child of light—involves abandoning everything to God: what others think of us, what others' harmful motives might be, fears about what others might do to us, hopes for getting ahead. We come to truly believe that God "knows what he's doing, and he'll keep on doing it" (1 Peter 4:19, MSG).

⌘ TODAY'S EXPERIMENT ⌘

Skim through the above *Renovation of the Heart* selection, "What Children of Light Are Like," and the previous one, "Children of Light."

Underline the phrases that describe the results you would most like to see in the dimensions of yourself—perhaps having a mind centered on God, not indulging thoughts of failure and hopelessness, or not thinking first of yourself. Or it might be having a tongue that is constantly poised to say what is loving and good without thinking, being completely transparent or effortless in the way you are.

Why do you want these things? How would they make your life more meaningful? What would be your next steps (spiritual disciplines)?

54

PROGRESSION OF SPIRITUAL GROWTH

The progression of spiritual growth starts from the bedrock of God's "divine power [that] has granted to us *everything* pertaining to life and godliness." (2 Peter 1:3, emphasis added). God's "precious and magnificent promises" make it possible for us to "become partakers of the divine nature, having escaped the corruption that is in the world by lust" (1:4).

This escape comes about by putting forth our best efforts ("applying all diligence," 2 Peter 1:5) to add the following things to our confidence in Christ (see 2 Peter 1:5-7):

- *Moral excellence* or virtue. Train yourself to do what is good and right.
- *Knowledge* or understanding. Come to know why the good and right you do *is* good and right.
- *Self-control.* Develop the capacity to carry out your intentions and not be thrown off by any turn of events.
- *Perseverance* (endurance, patience). Demonstrate the capacity to stick with the course over the long haul regardless of how you may feel.
- *Godliness.* Strive for depth and thoroughness in the preceding attainments of grace.
- *Brotherly kindness* and gentleness of care seen among siblings and true friends. Extend family feeling and action to those in your community. Think of what that would mean to this

wounded world. This superhuman thing is possible only through the goodness and strength of godliness.

- *Agape love.* Offer the kind of love that characterizes God himself and is spelled out in heartrending detail on the cross of Jesus and in 1 Corinthians 13. We are not to love simply as family but as he loved us (see John 13:34).

If we do these things, we will "never stumble," and "entrance into the eternal kingdom of our Lord and Savior Jesus Christ will be *abundantly* supplied to [us]" (2 Peter 1:10-11, emphasis added).

The mistake believers most commonly make is to assume they are supposed to do all these glowing things apart from inner transformation into Christlikeness, without loving God with all their heart, soul, mind, and strength in all the dimensions of the self. In fact, they think they must do them while they are still strongly inclined in the opposite direction, against God. To the person who is not inwardly transformed in each essential dimension, evil and sin still *look good.* But sin looks stupid, ridiculous, and repulsive to those cleansed by Christ who see the law as a beautiful gift of God, as precious truth about what is really good and right.

This list in 2 Peter can be overwhelming if we make it about us. One way we do that is to *try* to do these things, emphasizing *trying* instead of *training.* If we try to do these things, our efforts will be about us. We will berate ourselves when we fail; we will feel self-satisfied when we get something right. But as all our dimensions are trained by the Spirit through spiritual disciplines, we can increasingly connect with God throughout the day. The spiritual life then remains God-focused. It isn't about us.

Another skewed emphasis is when we get wrapped up in the formulaic rather than the relational. When we think, *If I do A, God will do B,* we're thinking of our own performance. But our focus must always be on God and our relationship to God. The important issue is continually putting our confidence in God as he delights in bringing us along on this journey of transformation in his kingdom. We're not performing—we're just tagging along behind Jesus, copying his fascinating way of *being*.

⚘ TODAY'S EXPERIMENT ⚘

Go back through this book and notice the things you have marked with your initials as next steps (see introduction)—perhaps ways to pray, dedicating your body. Pick out a few steps and examine how each one would help you connect with God and so move you down the road toward becoming a person who exhibits moral excellence, knowledge, self-control, perseverance, godliness, brotherly kindness, and *agape* love.

TO *BE* CHILDREN
OF LIGHT NOW

An accurate history of the nineteenth and twentieth centuries must indicate that the highest ethical teaching the world has ever known was rejected in favor of teachings that opened the way to forms of human behavior more degraded than any the world had seen to that point—from the Soviet form of communism to Hitler's fascist state, from Maoism to Pol Pot. Each pled moral righteousness as the justification for brutalities that no one would have thought possible. This is partly due to *the failure of those who have professed Christ to stand throughout the earth as the manifest children of light.*

Recent intellectual leaders have lived in an attitude of superiority and condemnation toward Christian morality. At the present time, popular culture has taken over the attack. Lyrics of the past did not critique traditional (Christian) teachings, but that changed with the Beatles and Bob Dylan. The bitterness of the previous generation's literary writings broke through. They professed to have *seen through* "the establishment," and they found much there to criticize justly. They promoted a "higher" morality to replace what they took to be "the establishment." Darkness was then said to be light.

Practicing what traditionally would have been regarded as blatant evil is now the single most dominant feature of our world. Sex and violence in the media is one symptom but is far from being the central issue. The central issue is the replacement of Jesus Christ as the Light of the World by people like Nietzsche and John Lennon, Lenin and Mao.

Children of light are beyond the point where *mere talk*—no matter how sound it is—can make an impression. Demonstration is required. They must live what they talk, even in places where they cannot talk what they live. The children of light must *be* who and what they were called to be by Christ their Head. Mere reason and fact cannot effectively persuade because they are now under the same sway of public spirit and institutions as are the arts and public life generally—and, indeed, so is much of the "church visible." The call of Christ today is to be his apprentices, alive in the power of God, learning to do all he said to do, leading others into apprenticeship to him, and teaching them how to do everything he said.

As Christians live an increasingly "ghettoized" lifestyle in which we go to aerobics classes, join bowling leagues, and use the Yellow Pages, we are forgetting that we can "live what we talk, even in places where we cannot talk what we live." Being involved in professional groups, community organizations, and sports teams that are not explicitly Christian, we can be children of salt and light who don't think of ourselves first, who aren't trapped by the unloving comments our tongues make before we think. We can be transparent people who lead an organization without manipulating and managing people. When we're urged to do something wrong, we can quietly refuse without being self-righteous. When accused, we can avoid defending ourselves and say only what is needed for clarity. We can show love and compassion to the people in the group who are in need. Neither sarcasm nor guilt-producing talk will come out of our mouth.

☙ TODAY'S EXPERIMENT ☙

Think of a group you are a part of that is not explicitly Christian—maybe your condo organization or neighborhood. Pick one person in that group and bring that person before God. Ask God to show you that person's heart. What does he need? What is her soul crying out for? How might you weep or rejoice with that person?

If someone insults or injures you, pray for God's help to demonstrate Christ's love in turning the other cheek, not taking offense easily or quickly, giving grace to others who may not be grace-filled themselves. Pray that God will give you opportunities to demonstrate the genuine, radiant love of God in simple, common ways.

56

THE DISTRACTED CHURCH

Churches that cause children of light to emerge and mature have turned their efforts under God toward making spiritual formation in Christlikeness their primary goal. The reason most congregations fail to routinely produce children of light is distraction. While majoring in minors, they become distracted by things the New Testament says nothing about. They devote most of their thought and effort to sermons, Sunday school, style of music, denominations, camps, or board meetings. *Those matters are not primary and will take care of themselves when what is primary is appropriately cared for.*

Such matters are "vessels" but are mistaken for the "treasure." The apostle Paul made a distinction between the vessels (or "jars of clay," our body, 2 Corinthians 4:7, NIV) and the treasure ("the Light of the knowledge of the glory of God in the face of Christ," 4:6). We might also apply this "vessel" distinction to the *practices, traditions,* and *groupings* to which many congregations devote their attention and effort. Many groups have become nearly 100 percent vessel. Often there is much good associated with these vessels, but we mistake them for the treasure: the real presence of Jesus Christ in our midst, living with increasing fullness in every essential dimension of the personality of the individual devoted to him as Savior and Teacher.

We debate: Should there be prayer ministry, and should it be part of the service, after the service, or at a different service? Should we be seeker friendly or whatever the alternatives are? How should we raise funds for the church, and how should they be spent? Such things are not unimportant, but they are not the foundational matters. And that is why the New Testament says nothing about them.

Many would-be children of light regret that they don't have a greater connectedness with God, that more of God's light isn't pouring through them. Some are shocked to consider that they have let a life of church activities be their substitute for having a life with God. They are so focused on organizing groups, dissecting the personality of the pastor, or increasing the church building's parking capacity that immersing themselves and others in the presence of our Trinitarian God rarely crosses their mind.

A program, in particular, can easily become a vessel. We become loyal to it; we give our money and time to see it continue. Meanwhile, we acknowledge the treasure—the real presence of Jesus Christ in our midst—but don't focus on it. A church that concentrates on the treasure isn't as likely to borrow successful programs from other churches. Instead, apprentices of Jesus in such a church get on their faces before God and ask him to show them how to immerse others in God. Even if the result looks something like an existing program, it will be administered from very different hearts when it comes out of the church's life with God.

‌ TODAY'S EXPERIMENT ‌

Speak to God about the vessels you hold dear. Perhaps you've attended a certain Bible study for many years and it has become, frankly, your life with God. Perhaps you're devoted to a certain program, a certain teacher, or a certain work of service. Is this vessel in some way eclipsing God, who is speaking to you today?

Consider what God may be telling you about this vessel—how God might become the life and breath within it or how you might examine your loyalty to it or even perhaps discard it as an important consideration in your life.

57

THE COSTS
OF NONDISCIPLESHIP

If a church spends most of its time on vessels, those who regularly attend will not progress in spiritual formation. These vessel matters do *not* bring anyone into Christlikeness. In fact, *standing on these things as important or essential is what produces mean and angry Christians. They have failed to aim toward becoming people who have the character of Christ.*

Such righteous meanness among Christians is a common point of commiseration among Christian leaders. A denominational leader recently asked me, "Why are Christians so mean?" The answer is that Christians are taught by word and example that it is more important to be right (in terms of their vessel or practice) than it is to be Christlike. Being right licenses a person to be mean—righteously mean, of course.

Now I must say something you can be mad at *me* about. A fundamental mistake of the conservative side of much of the Western church is that its *basic* goal is to get people into heaven rather than to get heaven into people. This creates groups of people who may be ready to die but clearly are not ready to live. They rarely can get along with one another, much less with those "outside." Often their most intimate relations are tangles of reciprocal harm, coldness, and resentment—righteous meanness. They have become "Christian" without being Christlike.

The way to get as many people into heaven as you can is to get heaven into as many people as you can—that is, to follow the path of genuine spiritual transformation or full-throttle discipleship to Jesus Christ. When we are counting results, we need to remember the many people (surrounded by churches) who will *not* be in heaven because they have never, to their knowledge, seen the reality of Christ in a living human being. These lives of the "converted" testify against the reality of "the life that is life indeed" (1 Timothy 6:19, PAR).

While volunteering in my community, I frequently meet people with generous hearts who aren't Christians. Typically, they used to belong to a church, but squabble after squabble erupted about music or the way an immature youth pastor was "terminated." They walked out the back door, never to return, but they were still hungry for Jesus. Somehow all that church activity had little to do with discipleship to Jesus. This is one of the costs of nondiscipleship in the church. Because people aren't focused on transformation into Christlikeness, they behave in ways that oppose Christ.

This often happens because of the focus on the so-called success of a program or the church. We begin by being irritated with someone who doesn't read the books we read or listen to the same music. We think, *They don't get what's important!* Then it becomes, *They don't care about evangelism* (or whatever our concern is). Implementing change or organizing a program is somehow more important than loving others.

More important than whether the music is "right" is whether the people on the worship team or in the choir love each other. More important than having capable staff members is whether they love and respect each other. It's a strange thought to some Christians that the most important thing about any meeting at church is not what is accomplished or decided but whether the participants treat each other with the love of Christ.

☙ TODAY'S EXPERIMENT ☜

Think of an area you feel certain you're right about and others just don't get. Pick one of those "others." Ask God to show you how to pray for that person. What would it look like to have the heart of Christ toward her—to speak the truth with great love? Or maybe to be quiet with great love? Consider whether pride is blocking the movement of love in you (for example, being a know-it-all).

58

God's Plan for Spiritual Formation

Many professing Christians today have a flawed view of what it is to have faith in Christ. They have "prayed to receive Christ" because they felt a need and want Jesus' help. But addressing "felt needs" cannot lay a foundation for spiritual formation because that is rarely the real problem. The problem is they have rejected God and not surrendered their will to him. They do not want to do what God says to do but rather what *they* think is best. They are "lost" in the sense explained earlier. They do not think they need the grace of God for radical transformation of who they are; they just need a little help.

Hopefully they will encounter churches that naturally produce children of light because they follow Jesus' instructions: "As you go throughout the world, make apprentices to me from all kinds of people, immerse them in Trinitarian reality, and teach them to do everything I have commanded you" (Matthew 28:19-20, PAR). These instructions are bookended by categorical statements about the plentiful resources for this undertaking: "I have been given say over everything in heaven and earth" and "Look, I'm with you every moment, until the work is done" (verses 18,20, PAR).

This is *Jesus' plan for spiritual formation in the local congregation*. It has three stages:

1. *Making disciples*, that is, *apprentices*, of Jesus. The New Testament does not recognize a category of Christians who are not apprentices of Jesus Christ in kingdom living, though

it recognizes "baby" apprentices who are still predominantly preoccupied with and dependent upon natural human abilities ("carnal").

2. *Immersing the apprentices at all levels of growth in the Trinitarian presence.* This is the single major component of the prospering of the local congregation: the healing and teaching God in their midst.

3. *Transforming disciples* inwardly in such a way that *doing the words and deeds of Christ is not the focus but is the natural outcome or side effect.* This is what "teaching them to do everything I have commanded you" amounts to.

Some wish Jesus had left behind a step-by-step program for discipleship. While we have the focus and instructions in Matthew 28:18-20, no specific methods are identified. But Jesus is the one who disciples people. You and I just need a general outline so we can be receptive to how God is using us in his process of discipleship. Discipleship is about relationship, so the process will be different for everyone. You and I get to pray and look deeply into the hearts of the people God brings us alongside.

☙ TODAY'S EXPERIMENT ❧

Think of someone you have wanted to influence for God. Maybe you don't think of yourself as "discipling" them, which is okay, because Jesus is the one who disciples people. Ask God to show you what the next step is with that person, perhaps using some of these questions:

- How well does this person comprehend the magnificence of the life of Jesus?
- What doubts fill his mind?
- What blocks her understanding?
- What might he be afraid of?
- How are you, O God, nudging her forward in purpose?

Consider how God may be calling you to minister to this person. Does he need you to simply call him and see how he's doing, or is there something specific you should invite him to do with you?

Think also about the activities you're involved in—not only specifically Christian ones but also your work and interaction in your neighborhood and family. How is God calling you to look at those around you as people he is apprenticing? What might you pray for a few of them?

STAGE ONE: MAKING APPRENTICES

Apprentices are those who have trusted Jesus with their whole life, so far as they understand it. They want to learn everything Jesus has to teach them about life in the kingdom of God and are constantly *with him* to learn to be like him.

First, they are learning to *understand* and *do* the things Jesus gave us specific commandments and teachings about. They study his words and deeds in the four Gospels. They explore what it means to give a cup of cold water to a little child in the name of Jesus (see Matthew 10:42), to not swear (see James 5:12), to love their enemies and pray for those who persecute them (see Matthew 5:44), and so forth. They are learning how to *actually do* these things.

The second aspect of discipleship concerns learning *how Jesus would lead our lives if he were in our place*. How would Jesus (living your life) get along with neighbors, participate in government, get an education, and engage in the cultural life of your society? *How would he do those things* if he were you? In these matters of ordinary human existence, Jesus is our constant teacher, and we are his constant apprentices. "He walks with me and he talks with me," as the old hymn says.

When setting out as his apprentices, we will sharply encounter all of the harmful things that are in us: false thoughts and feelings, self-will, bodily inclinations to evil, ungodly social relationships and patterns, and soul wounds and misconnections. Our Savior and Teacher will help us remove these as we strive forward through the many-sided ministries of himself, his kingdom, and his people. All will be bathed in the Holy Spirit.

The process of spiritual formation in Christlikeness is a process through which all the dimensions of our lives are transformed as they increasingly take on the character of our Teacher.

Perhaps the idea that apprentices "are constantly *with him* to learn to be like him" sounds too challenging to you. How could you accomplish this? Consider that the one who said, "I am with you always" (Matthew 28:20) is already by your side and may be doing things to get your attention. Our job, then, is to pay attention to this constant companion of our lives. This practice of the presence of God is not a chore but the best way to live. We can turn our thoughts to Jesus throughout the day, using small reminders at first but always living out of a foundation of regular moments of *being with* Jesus through the written Word (and this is the purpose of Bible reading—not just to get to the bottom of the page). To *be with* Jesus this way means that during such times we live in our heart as well as our head. Both are good, but insights aren't enough. We need to put our whole self into it and pray back to God what we find there. With gospel passages in particular, we can enter into them and tell Jesus how we respond to what we experience there.

Perhaps even more challenging is how apprentices are learning to lead their everyday lives as he would lead their lives if he were they. If you're a hair stylist or an engineer, how would Jesus do his work and treat his clients/coworkers if he were you? If you're an adult child of an aging parent or the parent of an uncooperative teenager, how would Jesus treat this person if he were in your shoes? If you're a small-business owner, how would Jesus approach your promotional activities? How would he respond to a complaining customer or times a product failed to measure up? What would Jesus write in each e-mail if he were in your body, living your life, responding to the person who just e-mailed you?

ᢙᔎ TODAY'S EXPERIMENT ᢙᔎ

What is your next step in *understanding* and *doing* the things Jesus gave
us specific commandments and teachings about? Consider *how Jesus
would lead your life if he were you*—working at your job, living in your
family and neighborhood, going to your church.

60

ARRANGING FOR TRANSFORMATION

The second stage in God's plan for the growth and prospering of local congregations has to do with *immersing the apprentices into the Trinitarian presence*. God's intent is to be present among his people and heal them, teach them, and provide for them. A local congregation of disciples of Jesus should be *a place where divine life and power is manifestly present to glorify God and meet the needs of repentant human beings*. This implies an atmosphere of honesty, openness, indiscriminate acceptance of all, and supernatural caring with utter admiration for and confidence in Jesus.

Performance, which is where we try to make an impression rather than just be what we are, would be absent in the Trinitarian gathering, as would constant solicitude concerning "How did the service go?" God is the primary agent in the gathering. From the only point of view that matters (God's), no human knows how the service went. The minister does not need techniques but needs only speak Christ's Word *from Christ's character*, standing within the manifest presence of God.

The third stage, intending and *arranging for the inner transformation of disciples*, is what Jesus described as teaching the disciples to do all he commanded. The *doing* of what he commanded is not the focus of our activities at this point; rather, it is the natural outcome or side effect. The focus is inner transformation of the five essential aspects of human personality that we have been studying. This should be the local congregation's constant preoccupation.

If this is your congregation, *announce* that you teach people to do the things that Jesus said to do. Publicize and run training programs designed to develop specific points of the character of Christ as given in the New Testament. Put the whole weight of the staff and the congregation toward this effort.

All of the other details of church activities will matter little, one way or the other, so long as all are *organized around* God's plan for spiritual formation in the local congregation.

Imagine the classes offered at such a church: being genuinely kind to hostile people, returning blessing for cursing, living without contempt, living without lust, speaking simply (see Matthew 5). In order to change the dimensions of the self so that these behaviors grow from within, such classes include time for questions and discussion so that students can offer ideas of what these behaviors look like (discipline of *community*). Students do exercises from Scripture to envision how Jesus did these things (*study, meditation*). They then role-play these situations and offer testimonies of successes and failures (*confession, prayer, celebration*).

What happens in such a class is . . . nearly magical. Attendees get a taste of who Jesus is and what it looks like to walk and talk like Jesus. They begin to grieve their sarcastic comebacks and manipulative speech. Apologies occur among participants regarding that last heated discussion about the church budget. Jesus becomes the center of attention as all begin wondering, *How would Jesus live his life if he were in my shoes?*

ᴥ TODAY'S EXPERIMENT ᴥ

Reflect on Jesus in this scene: On the *Via Dolorosa*, as Jesus carried his cross and suffered the effects of mental and physical torture, he noticed among the crowd following him some women who mourned and wailed for him. In this moment (where I would have been self-consumed), he turned to them in great concern about their future:

"Daughters of Jerusalem, do not weep for me; weep for yourselves and for your children" (Luke 23:28, NIV). He warned them of the impending horror of the destruction of Jerusalem.

Imagine these women years later remembering his words and saving themselves and their children. Jesus never stopped looking out for other people. A few hours later he could naturally say, "Father, forgive them; for they do not know what they are doing" (Luke 23:34).

When I'm suffering, I struggle not to think that everything is about me, yet Jesus in his great need turned to address the needs and hurts of others! O Jesus, help us have the kind of heart that naturally turns to comfort and help others.

If you wish, turn to Luke 23:27-31 and review what comes before it. Consider what it would be like to have this heart of Christ. What does this experience make you want to pray to God?

MOVING FORWARD

The path of renovation of the heart is one in which the revitalized will takes grace-provided measures to change the content of the thought life, the dominant feeling tones, what the body is ready to do, the prevailing social atmosphere, and the deep currents of the soul. These all are to be progressively transformed *toward* the character they each have in Jesus Christ.

Willpower is not the key to personal transformation. Rather, the will and character progress in effectual well-being and well-doing only as *all other essential aspects of the person* come into line with the intent of a will brought to newness of life from above by the Word and the Spirit.

Now is the time for specific planning. Are there areas where our will is not abandoned to God's will or where old segments of fallen character remain unchallenged? Do some of our thoughts, images, or patterns of thinking show more of our kingdom or the kingdom of evil than they do God's kingdom—for example, as they relate to money or social practices or efforts to bring the world to Christ? Is our body still our master in some area? Are we its servant rather than it ours?

And if we have some role in leadership among Christ's people, are we doing all we reasonably can to aid and direct their progress in inward transformation into Christlikeness? Is that progress the true aim of our lives together, and are there ways in which our activities might be more supportive of that aim? Is the teaching that goes out from us appropriate to the condition of the people, and is our example one that gives clear assurance and direction? Is "our progress evident to all"? (1 Timothy 4:15, PAR).

Spiritual formation in Christlikeness is the sure outcome of well-directed activities that are under the personal supervision of Christ and are sustained by all of the instrumentalities of his grace. This aching world is waiting for the people explicitly identified with Christ to be, through and through, the people he intends them to be.

"Christ in you, the hope of glory" is possible (Colossians 1:27, NIV). Christ can live in all the dimensions of you. God's grace will do it, but God wants your cooperation.

❧ TODAY'S EXPERIMENT ❧

Consider how God may be leading you as you've worked through this book to focus your *mind* on the things of Christ—to examine the ideas and images you picture there; to ponder Scripture in a slow, full way; to read material that stretches you; to memorize a passage that describes who you need to be. (Review devotions 21–26 if you wish.)

Consider how God is leading you to examine where you routinely let your *feelings* dwell—to investigate what ideas and images guide your feelings; to cultivate feelings of faith, hope, and love, which build the underlying conditions of love, joy, and peace (devotions 27–32).

Consider how God is leading you to examine your *character* based on what automatically slips out without your thinking about it—to explore where you are on the continuum of identifying your *will* with God's (surrender, abandonment, contentment, participation in accomplishing God's will in our world); to ask God what spiritual disciplines would help you align your will with his (devotions 33–36).

Consider how God is leading you to review what you discovered about what your *body* is poised to do—to walk through the steps of releasing your body to God if you did not do so and to review it if you did (devotion 39); to admit ways you have idolized your body or misused it to dominate or manipulate others; to arrange your life for rest and Sabbath (devotions 37–41).

Consider how God is leading you in your *social dimension*—to review your sense of ease or lack of ease at being reciprocally rooted in others; to admit the routine ways of attack and withdrawal you have continued to discover about yourself; to pray that God will work "genuine love" in you (devotions 42–46).

Consider how God is leading you to review the kinds of things you routinely say to your *soul* and that your soul cries out—to abandon outcomes in humility to God; to embrace the teachings of Scripture (law) as sweetness and light (devotions 47–51).

RETREATING

Perhaps you'd like to use this book to do your own personal retreat, but you're not sure how. Here are some guidelines for having a personal retreat and some suggestions for how you might focus the retreat on areas in your life discussed in *Renovation of the Heart in Daily Practice*.

GUIDELINES FOR A PERSONAL RETREAT

If you are embarking on a personal retreat, congratulations! This is what Jesus did regularly, and I believe he really looked forward to those times.

One of the purposes of a retreat is for you to interact with God, so you want to promote that kind of conversation. Hopefully this book will bring forth ideas that God wants you to consider. Responding to God is very important—it's not a conversation unless you respond. And God really likes hearing from you!

Here are some tips to help you:

- Don't be surprised if you feel lost once you get settled in. You may even question yourself: *Why am I here, and what gave me the crazy idea I could take off from all my responsibilities to sit here and do nothing?* Don't let this bother you. If Jesus needed a forty-day retreat, you're okay in taking a few days or hours to retreat.
- Don't be a martyr when taking a personal retreat. Be comfortable. Unless you've done quite a bit of this, don't fast at the same time.
- Bring a journal. If journaling intimidates you, call it scribbling. Don't worry about spelling and grammar—just let it flow. You

don't have to write a lot, but make some notes about what comes to you. Ideally, a journal entry will begin with, "Dear God . . ." Writing the prayers is helpful because otherwise prayer can become just muddling over things. When you write it, you think more precisely. You may be very surprised at times by what you write. Truths about your deeper self may flow unexpectedly. Watch for that.

- Schedule yourself loosely. You can adhere to the "sittings" structure such as the one below, but it shouldn't rule you. The retreat was made for you; you weren't made for the retreat (as Jesus worded the Sabbath principle in Mark 2:27).

- Address feelings of resistance. You may get into the material and find that you'd much rather think or talk *about* God than actually speak *to* God. At that point, it's best to admit that to yourself and perhaps laugh about it. It might help to change venue, however. Take this book or your journal and go for a walk. Continue to mildly pray about your interaction with God and see what else comes to you.

- Break up your retreat time into "sittings" (or sessions). Normally these should not be longer than an hour; stop while you're still enjoying it. Consider these sessions "prayer periods" — times of more formal interaction with God. Sittings might take this flow: Read a selection and then do "Today's Experiment." If you finish one, do the next one. Don't be concerned about how many you finish. Some might move quickly; others you may even want to repeat. Journal as needed.

- Between sessions, enjoy doing something that doesn't require concentration, such as taking a walk or hike. Using the right brain is particularly helpful here: Do woodworking or stitchery; paint pictures; listen to orchestral music (classical or wordless soundtracks) or Taizé worship (soft, meditative music); look through a book of great art. If you have worship music with you and a certain song is resonating with you, play that as well. Do not do anything that distracts you (checking e-mail and so on). Even reading a novel or watching a video will change the train of thought God has you on. (I do, however, recommend the DVD *The Gospel of John.*) The point is that you do not want to interrupt the flow of your conversation with God.

A SPECIALIZED FOCUS FOR THE RETREAT

Jumpstart focus. You may use this retreat to begin talking to God about renovating your heart. Start at the beginning of the book and move at a pace that suits you (see further instructions below). When you return home, continue as you've started. Be sure to keep your notes from the retreat to reflect upon.

Since you won't be able to get through the entire set of devotions, you may want to focus narrowly on a certain topic that is central for you:

- *VIM.* Devotions 17–20 introduce the VIM pattern (vision, intention, means). Devotions 21 and 26 also mention the VIM pattern in relation to the renovation of the mind. In addition, devotions 52–55 brilliantly portray the vision (V) in the idea of our becoming children of light.
- *Ruined Life and Restored Life.* Consider using devotions 10–13 to look at the way our self-preoccupied life is typically lived. Then move on to devotions 14–16, which focus on the restored life, which is life in the kingdom of God here and now. This latter section is really about death to self, an all-important topic rarely mentioned today.
- *Healing for Damaged Emotions.* Spiritual formation is difficult for people who have suffered emotional trauma or have been ruled by their emotions. A retreat setting is an ideal place to focus on this, using devotions 27–32. Besides these devotions, you may want to use favorite psalms or memorize Romans 5:1-8.
- *Healing for My Thought Life.* Since the first freedom is where you put your mind, you may want to focus an entire retreat on this central issue. Use devotions 21–26 (noting how the mind affects the emotions) and devotions 27–32, perhaps memorizing Colossians 3:1-17.
- *Transforming the Will.* If you feel that nothing will ever change,

you might want to focus on devotions 33–36. They emphasize spiritual disciplines, so you might want to take books on that topic along for further study. Also, if you are confused about why the heart, will, and spirit are the same, take a concordance and enjoy studying that.

- *Transforming the Body.* Devotions 37–41 help you look at how your body has been captive to responses that betray both you and Jesus. Because the important ritual in devotion 39 (dedicating the body) is easily set aside, a retreat is an ideal time to do it without hurrying.

- *Transforming the Social Dimension.* If relationships (or just people in general!) are troubling you, devotions 42–46 allow you to step back and look at how God is working with you. Though some exercises aren't doable in solitude, your solitary pondering of them at such a distance may be an advantage.

- *Transforming the Soul.* Talking to one's soul (aloud) in the style of Psalm 103 may be awkward for you at home, but a retreat provides you with the privacy to try it (devotion 48). Devotions 47–51 provide more of what you need to do that.

- *Transforming the Body of Christ.* If you're concerned about your local church and want to pray and ponder how spiritual formation might work there, use your retreat to move through devotions 56–61. Again, use the section on the children of light to give you a vision of what is possible (devotions 52–55).

Notes

1. C. S. Lewis, *An Experiment in Criticism* (Cambridge, UK: Cambridge University Press, 1961), 88–89.
2. Walter Trobisch, *Martin Luther's Quiet Time* (Downers Grove, IL: InterVarsity, 1975), 3, 7–10.
3. For development of this understanding, please see chapters 1–3 of Dallas Willard, *The Divine Conspiracy* (San Francisco: HarperSanFrancisco, 1998).
4. See C. S. Lewis's discussion of "The Inner Ring" and the desire to be in it as "one of the permanent mainsprings of human action." *The Weight of Glory* (Grand Rapids, MI: Eerdmans, 1973), 61.

About the Authors

DALLAS WILLARD is a professor and former director of the School of Philosophy at the University of Southern California. He received his PhD from the University of Wisconsin. Dallas is the author of more than thirty publications, including *The Divine Conspiracy*, *The Spirit of the Disciplines* (both HarperSanFrancisco), and *Hearing God* (InterVarsity). He and his wife, Jane, live in Chatsworth, California. They have two children and one grandchild. Many of his writings in philosophy and religion are available from his web page, www.dwillard.org.

JAN JOHNSON is a writer, speaker, and spiritual director. She holds a DMin in Ignatian spirituality and spiritual direction. She is the author of more than one thousand magazine articles, truckloads of Bible study curricula, and fifteen books, including *Enjoying the Presence of God*, *When the Soul Listens*, *Savoring God's Word* (all NavPress), *Living a Purpose-Full Life* (WaterBrook Press), and the SPIRITUAL DISCIPLINES BIBLE STUDIES series (InterVarsity Press). She lives with her husband, Greg, in Simi Valley, California. They have two adult children. Her website, www.janjohnson.org, features many articles, book chapters, and her speaking schedule.

MORE LIFE-CHANGING BOOKS FROM DALLAS WILLARD.

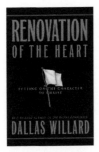

Renovation of the Heart

Dallas Willard
1-57683-296-1

We aren't born again to stay the way we are. Learn how to shed sinful habits and increasingly take on the character of Christ through "the transformation of the spirit," a personal apprenticeship with Jesus Christ.

Revolution of Character

Dallas Willard with Don Simpson
1-57683-857-9

Spiritual guide Dallas Willard helps readers reflect on the spiritual significance of each element of the human self, providing fresh and spiritually invigorating opportunities to meditate on Scripture.

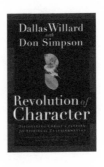

Renovation of the Heart: An Interactive Student Edition

Dallas Willard and Randy Frazee
1-57683-730-0

With easy-to-understand examples, review questions, and explanations of key words, this book helps us understand one of the most complicated and important lessons of life: putting on the character of Christ.

Visit your local Christian bookstore, call NavPress at 1-800-366-7788, or log on to www.navpress.com to purchase. To locate a Christian bookstore near you, call 1-800-991-7747.

BRINGING TRUTH TO LIFE
www.navpress.com